mi Comida Latina

VIBRANT · FRESH
SIMPLE · AUTHENTIC

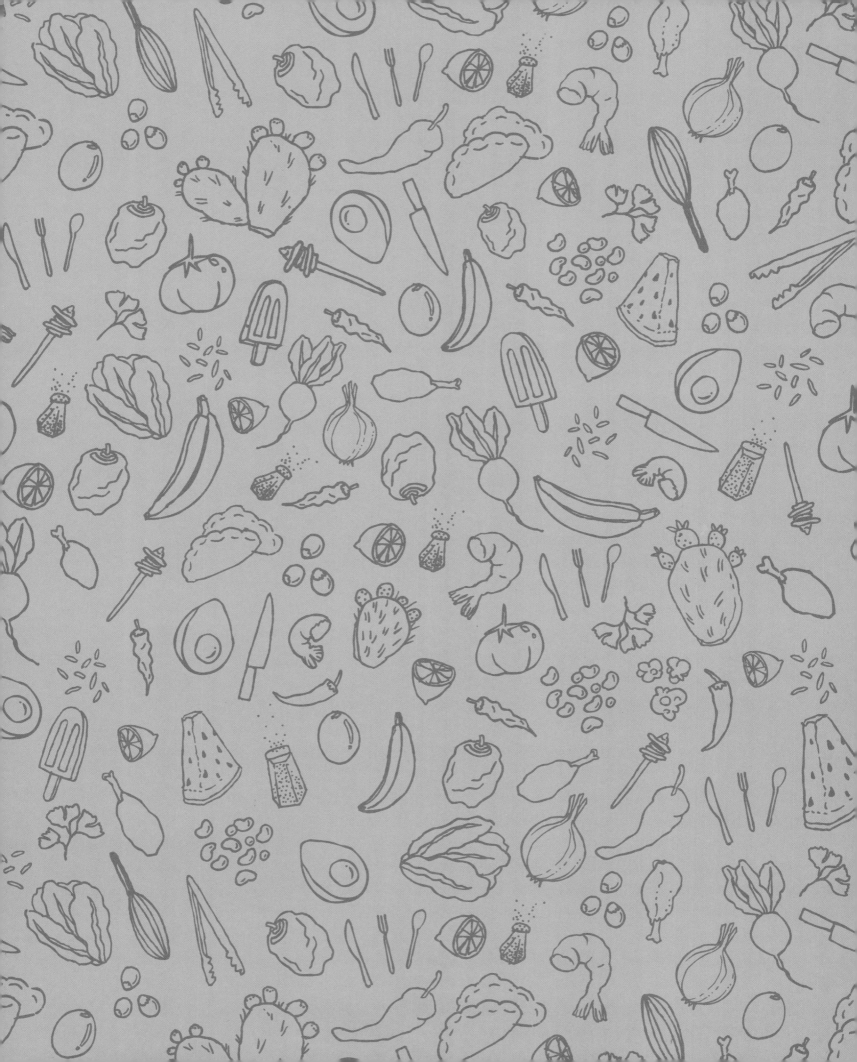

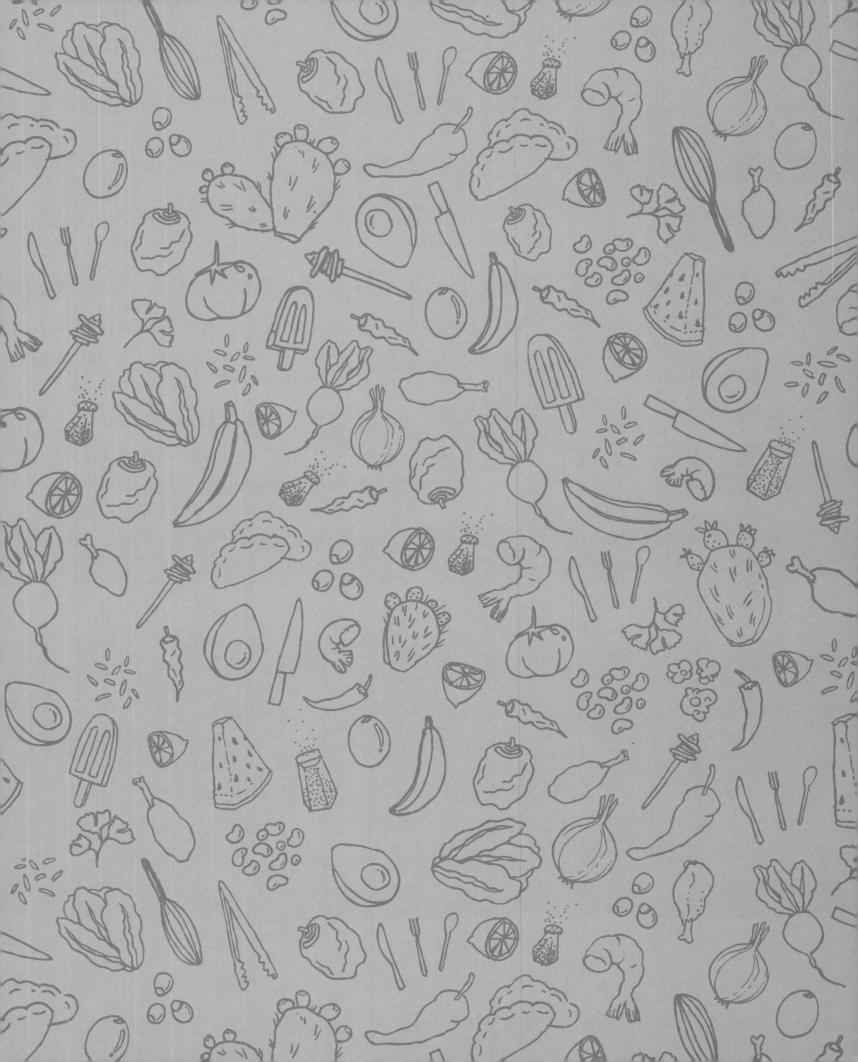

mi Comida Latina

VIBRANT · FRESH
SIMPLE · AUTHENTIC

Marcella Kriebel

Mi Comida Latina
Vibrant, Fresh, Simple, Authentic

Written, hand lettered & illustrated by Marcella Kriebel

Burgess Lea Press
New Hope, Pennsylvania
www.burgessleapress.com

2 3 4 5 6 7 8 9 10
Printed in China by 1010 Printing Group Limited

Book design by Marcella Kriebel
Edited by Kate Winslow

ISBN: 978-1-941868-01-0
Library of Congress PCN on file with the publisher

Burgess Lea Press donates 100 percent of our after-tax profits on each
book to culinary education, feeding the hungry, farmland preservation
& other food-related causes.

DEDICATED TO MY GRANDFATHERS

William B. Kriebel ARTIST & SELF PUBLISHER
Max Mack ARTIST & SIGN PAINTER

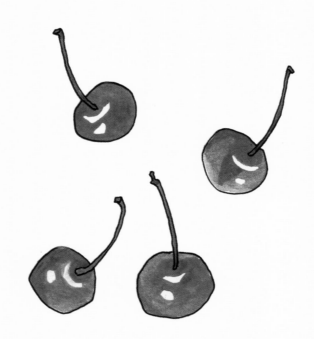

This cookbook contains authentic dishes
discovered during travel in Latin America
& original recipes inspired by
family & friends.

Over 100 hand drawn favorites

Plenty of GLUTEN FREE, VEGETARIAN
& VEGAN OPTIONS

Chicken, seafood & red meat
included

TABLE
of Contents

I grew up in a community of makers in a world where Do It Yourself was the norm. Cooking in our hand-built cob mud oven in the backyard, mixing up fresh pasta & putting up preserves were the kinds of activities enjoyed by my extended family & friends. We shared many meals comprised of wonderful fresh ingredients.

As a child, I went to a small school that prided itself on its cross-disciplinary education with a strong emphasis on project-oriented learning, art, music, performance & international studies. I learned the importance of following a concept through from start to finish.

Later, my anthropology studies at Willamette University in Oregon taught me how to look at the world through an ethnographic lens, & that the best way to understand people and their experiences is to immerse yourself in what they are doing — just as I had been doing all of my life. It is no surprise that when I started to travel as a teenager, I found myself making meals with my hosts. During my college years, travel in Latin America introduced me to new friends & their kitchens in several countries, from Oaxaca, Mexico, to Medellín, Colombia, enriching my experience & providing a window into these varied cultures. I continue to learn from my Latin American friends here in the US.

The recipes in this book began as a visual journal during my travels, as a way to record my food experiences. I started sketching pictures in the margins of my Spanish notes: the ingredients, techniques & preparation of each dish. I made a point of collecting recipes from home cooks & adding to my collection of authentic dishes wherever I went, filling several sketch books with recipes & drawings. The pages of this book represent the evolution of these original field notes into a more refined format.

When I make these dishes, I am transported back to the kitchens of Quito or San Miguel de Allende, where I originally learned how to prepare them. I am able to relive wonderful aromas & flavors — & memories — by recreating these dishes. I recall the quick hands of Marco Tulio Fiallo in

Ecuador as I slice onions or Rosa Sanabria's graceful manner of roasting chiles in hot oil. I think fondly of Lili's grandmother carefully explaining her technique for preparing Salvadoran-style chayote. I am so very grateful for the knowledge, generosity, & passion for food that these friends have shared with me.

I could not have predicted such an exciting chain of events when I set out to self-publish this book, & I must express my appreciation for the overwhelming support I received. In 2012, after losing my art installation position, I spent a year compiling these recipes & painting their accompanying illustrations with a tiny travel watercolor paint set. In October of that year, I shared my project on Kickstarter, through a video created by my friend Leslie Atkins, & in thirty days I made six times my monetary goal. This tremendous success on Kickstarter enabled me to produce 1,000 first-edition copies, then an additional printing of 1,200. Fast forward to now, with the help of Burgess Lea's talented team, I am sharing a bigger & better version of the book after selling out of my self-published edition.

In the following pages, you will find more than 100 of my favorite recipes from Latin America, all hand-lettered & illustrated. It is my hope that this book will inspire you to try new dishes in your own kitchen & explore some of the wonderful ingredients that may be unfamiliar to you, including yuca, prickly pear & epazote.

My culinary approach relies on taste, rather than strict measurements. My cooking mentors would suggest a pinch of this & a handful of that in sharing their recipes with me & I encourage readers to think of each page as a framework of flavors & colors that are always open to experimentation. Don't be afraid to substitute, or add a bit more of one ingredient or less of another according to your taste.

May we fondly remember our past journeys & look forward to those yet to come. And above all, may we keep sharing our passion for preparing delicious food!

buen provecho,
Marcella

Tips Tools & techniques

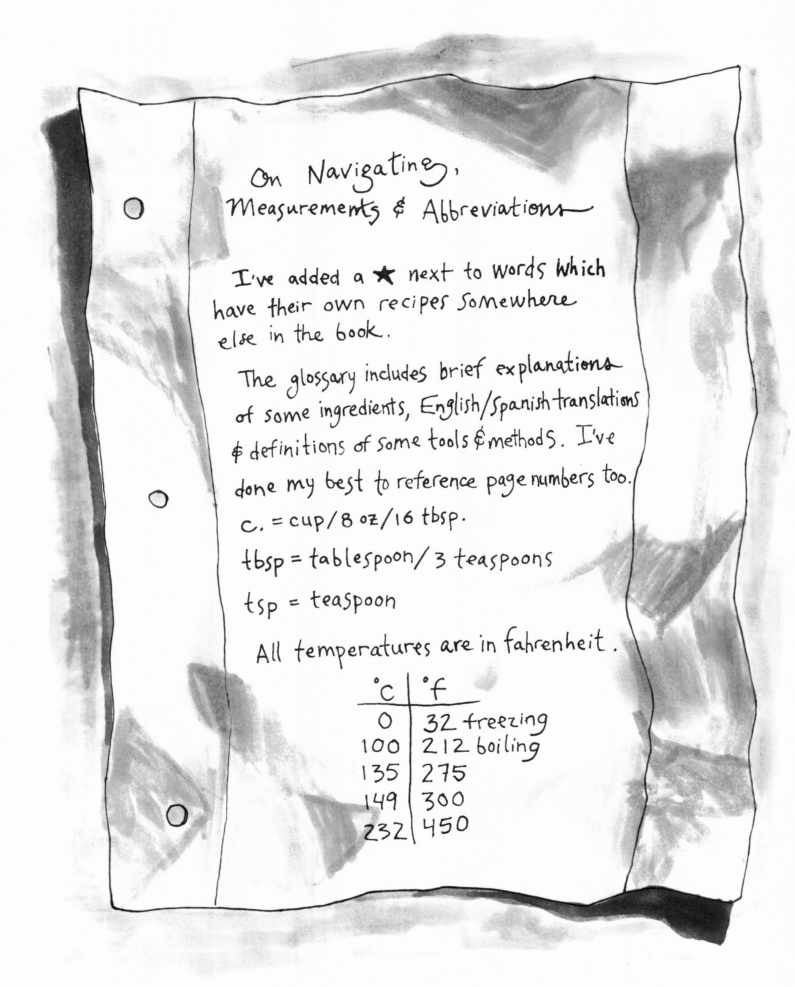

On Navigating, Measurements & Abbreviations

I've added a ★ next to words which have their own recipes somewhere else in the book.

The glossary includes brief explanations of some ingredients, English/Spanish translations & definitions of some tools & methods. I've done my best to reference page numbers too.

c. = cup/8 oz/16 tbsp.

tbsp = tablespoon/3 teaspoons

tsp = teaspoon

All temperatures are in fahrenheit.

°c	°f
0	32 freezing
100	212 boiling
135	275
149	300
232	450

Use real, fresh food to create the best food

AS A RULE OF THUMB, KNOW WHERE YOUR FOOD COMES FROM

Locally sourcing your ingredients not only helps support food growers in your community, it makes your dishes taste better too. Whenever you buy from the small farms in your area, you're standing up for fair labor practices & living wages for farm workers. You'll also be serving your family & friends more flavorful & nutritious produce, instead of the mass-produced fruits & veggies bred for the long shelf lives & expensive transportation required by supermarkets. You'll see & taste the difference in the depth of flavor, richness of color and improved texture of your meals.

At the supermarket, avoid products made with artificial ingredients or preservatives. Use real vanilla extract! Buy fresh handmade tortillas from a Latin American grocery. Use fresh-squeezed lime juice, & fresh herbs whenever possible.

¡Chile!

The spicy capsicum of the pepper family originated in the Americas, but has been a dynamic addition to food all over the world since the 15th century.

The flavors vary, depending on how the chile is prepared. A fresh marisol pepper is spicy & fruity. Dried, it becomes a rich & smoky guajillo. Similar to many chiles, this name change distinguishes fresh from dry.

CUTTING FRESH CHILES

Much of the heat from a chile is in the outer membrane of the seeds: removing the seeds will produce a milder flavor. The flesh is spicy, due to a chemical compound called CAPSAICIN. Wash hands thoroughly after cutting them or you will surely feel the burn later!

DRIED CHILE PREPARATION

Drying chiles intensifies their flavor so unlike fresh chiles, removing seeds does not alter a chile's spiciness. Ways to prepare dried chiles before adding them to your food include:

Grind them with a mortar & pestle or in a blender, creating a chile powder. Make sure to contain these spicy particles during this process; they can escape the vessel easily. Store in an air-tight container.

Soak dried chiles in warm water, crisp them in pan on stove or heat in olive oil before adding to your dish. Any of these methods will bring out the flavor & fragrance of the chile.

ROASTING & PEELING CHILES

See chiles rellenos recipe.

FRESH · ROASTED

DRIED · GROUND · PEELED

MAIZE

Widely cultivated as early as 3-5,000 BCE, maize has maintained its status as a culinary staple in Latin America & is used in many forms including:

MASA HARINA:
a type of corn flour made from a large kernel corn, posole, that has been soaked in lime or wood ash lye water. The kernels swell up & the hull becomes loose & is then discarded. The kernels are dried, then ground into masa harina. This process makes the dough softer & more elastic; it's called nixtamalization. Masa harina is used for tortillas & tamales & is best fresh.

CORN MEAL:
a dried ground corn available in a fine, medium & coarse grind used for many kinds of tortilla chips & corn bread. Arepas are often made from a precooked corn meal called "Masarepa".

Mexican Style Tortillas de Maíz
1-2 c. water, 2 c. masa harina, pinch of salt   YIELDS 15

In a large bowl, mix the water slowly into the masa & salt. Knead the dough for several minutes until smooth (not sticky or crumbly). Form a small ball & flatten in tortilla press.

Cook on comál or pan on both sides, serve warm.

add wax paper on both surfaces.

plantains: maduro y verde

Green plantains, known as "verde" (green) are starchy & firm & are used in countless dishes in Latin America. Let them sit around a week or two & they turn yellow with brown spots, known as "maduro" (mature). Spots are okay, underneath the ugly peel is the sweet, darker yellow maduro, which is featured in many recipes unique to the maduro.

Eating Cactus

Unlike most fruits, a *tuna*, the fruit of a prickly pear cactus, can be eaten at any stage of ripeness. The flesh of the green *tuna agria* (also known as *xoconostle*) is tender yet firm on the outside, making it an ideal choice for a salsa or pico de gallo.

A *tuna's* seeds are edible, but may seem a bit hard to sink your teeth into. Sometimes seeds can be difficult to separate from the *tuna's* flesh. In this case, you can process the flesh in a blender & then strain out the seeds. This process is often used to make juice using the purple, sweeter variety of the prickly pear.

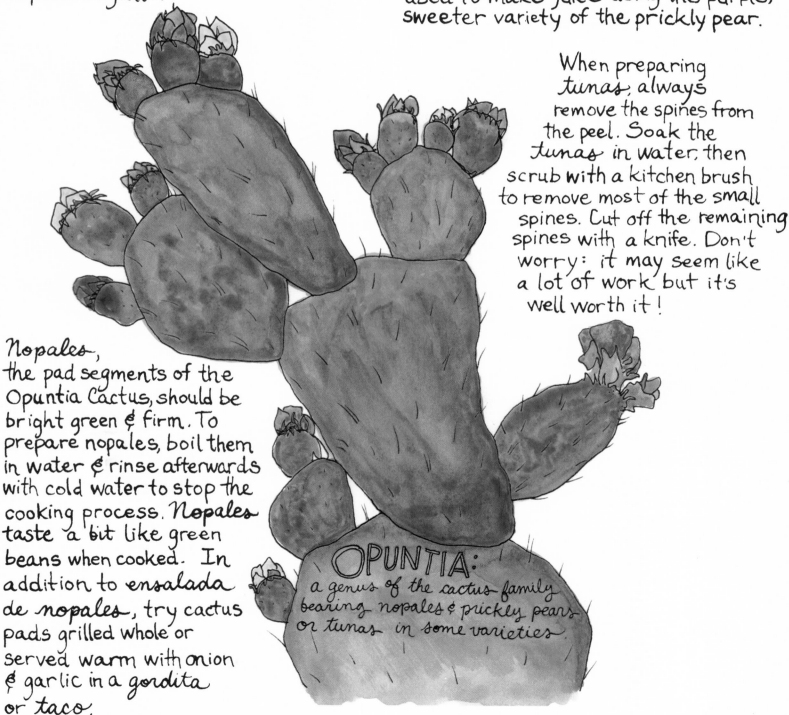

When preparing *tunas*, always remove the spines from the peel. Soak the *tunas* in water, then scrub with a kitchen brush to remove most of the small spines. Cut off the remaining spines with a knife. Don't worry: it may seem like a lot of work but it's well worth it!

Nopales, the pad segments of the Opuntia Cactus, should be bright green & firm. To prepare nopales, boil them in water & rinse afterwards with cold water to stop the cooking process. *Nopales* taste a bit like green beans when cooked. In addition to *ensalada de nopales*, try cactus pads grilled whole or served warm with onion & garlic in a *gordita* or *taco*.

OPUNTIA: a genus of the cactus family bearing nopales & prickly pears or tunas in some varieties.

SELECT THE BEST

Most Beautiful, Juicy, Flavorful Piece in the pile!

Many fruits will continue to ripen after being picked, including mangoes, pineapples, peaches & plums. If not eaten immediately, select your fruit a bit underripe.

To ripen, place fruit in a paper bag & keep at room temperature. To slowly ripen, refrigerate.

AVOCADO: Unlike many fruits, avocados start to ripen after they are picked. Ripe ones should be a little soft & the most soft around where the stem once was.

MELON: Should smell sweet. One w/o fragrance will not taste like much, either. Push the stem end. If ripe it should give a little.

CHAYOTE: Skin should be firm, light green & have no yellow or brown spots.

GUAVA: The Central American variety is little & green, about the size of an egg, they become sweeter & softer as they turn yellow.

PASSION FRUIT: In its ripe state, it should be slightly wrinkly & shades of yellow, red & pink.

PINEAPPLE: A whole fruit should smell sweet. Pluck a leaf out of the top of the pineapple. If it is ripe, it should come out with little effort. Always buy one that is at least part yellow, it will continue to ripen.

PAPAYA: Shake the whole fruit; you should hear the seeds bounce around inside. Flesh should be mostly yellow & soft. Be careful - it bruises easily.

MANGO: Regardless of the variety, fruit should be soft but not mushy & should smell sweet.

HOW TO EAT A MANGO WITHOUT PEELING OR SLICING OPEN FRUIT

Massage a ripe mango in your hands slowly, so not to break the peel. Once the pit feels like it is suspended freely in the pulp, remove the small bit where the stem was. Suck out the pulp!

FIG: The best figs are always picked fresh off the tree. They do not keep well & won't continue to ripen once picked. Figs are soft & are either dark purple, green or brown when ripe, depending on the variety.

WATERMELON: Thump the whole melon; if it sounds hollow, it is ripe. A ripe one usually has little contrast between the color of the stripes on the outside.

THUMP SMELL FEEL SHAKE LISTEN LOOK

A few WORDS ON some LATIN AMERICAN CHEESES

Ranging from crumbly & salty to soft & mild, Latin American cheeses vary in texture, flavor & use. Most are made from cow's milk & sometimes goat's milk. Some of the most commonly available varieties are listed below.

Queso Oaxaca/Quesillo: an elastic, stringy cheese that melts well. Made in a long rope shape & sold in a ball. Tastes creamy & mild. Similar to mozzarella. Use this cheese in Chiles Rellenos.

Requeson: a moist fresh spreadable cheese similar to ricotta. Complements berry jam or guava paste.

Crema: a runny cheese that is a little salty, like crème fraîche, but can be both sweet & sour. Often served on fish tacos, or spread on corn on the cob.

Queso fresco: a mild, fresh, soft & crumbly cheese used in soups and fillings. Milky tasting but not too rich. Similar to a mild feta.

Queso blanco: Similar in flavor to queso fresco, but this cow's milk cheese doesn't melt as easily. It becomes creamy & soft without losing its shape, which makes an it excellent frying cheese.

Panela: a soft, somewhat salty cheese usually showing the imprint of a basket mold. Absorbs other flavors well. I serve it on salads.

Cotija: a salty, crumbly cheese similar to a dry feta. I use this cheese on refried beans or mixed in a nopales salad.

Queso Añejo (meaning aged) Often made with goat's milk & has a paprika spice exterior. A more aged version of cotija, but not as salty. Shreds well.

Queso Botanero: a smooth, soft cheese that always has herbs, spices, or chiles in it. Serve as an appetizer.

Queso Palmita: a soft cheese that is salty & has lots of holes. Smooth & packed in water. Commonly known as queso blanco.

Asadera: A firm, slightly aged cheese, similar to provolone. Melts well. Good for quesadillas or grilling.

Manchego: Originating in Spain & traditionally made from sheep's milk, manchego is a popular choice in Mexico as a melting cheese. I like manchego served with membrillo paste.

1.

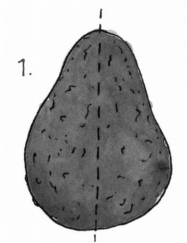

Cut avocado in half lengthwise.

An Efficient Way to Enjoy an Avocado
This way of removing the avocado seed is quick & clean. For best results, make sure the avocado is ripe.

2.

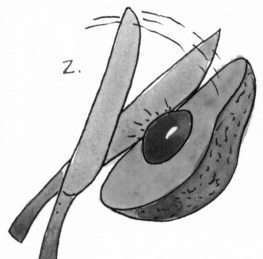

Firmly hit the seed with the sharp edge of the knife

3.

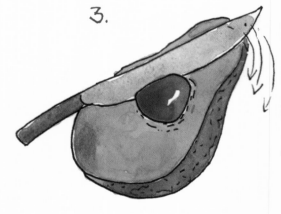

Rotate the knife to dislodge seed from the avocado.

4. Slice or scoop out the avocado flesh.

The Best Way to Cut an ONION

When I was in Ecuador, one of my dear elder hosts, Marco Tulio, taught me how to chop an onion, a skill that I have applied in my cooking ever since. Marco's method of keeping the root intact until the the end makes it easier to cut quickly into more uniform pieces as the root holds all the layers together.

1. Cut onion in half lengthwise.

2. Remove top & skin

3. Make lengthwise cuts from top to ⅛" from the root.

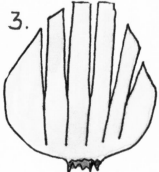

4. To chop, make crosswise cuts, leaving root until last.

How to Open a Coconut

First, pick a good one! A ripe coconut should have slightly darker eyes than the color of the shell, & you should be able to hear the coconut water slosh inside if you give it a shake.

1. Empty out the coconut water by piercing the eyes of the coconut with an awl or screwdriver. If necessary, use a hammer to tap on the end of the screwdriver to drive it through the shell.

2. On a griddle or pan, heat the whole coconut over high heat, rotating it so that it toasts evenly. You'll start to smell the delicious aroma of coconut. Within 5-10 minutes the hard outer shell will crack. Remove from the heat & cool for 10 min.

3. Put the coconut in a sealable bag, close it, & throw it down on the ground (outdoors on concrete) to break it into pieces.
Repeat if necessary.

4. Remove the coconut meat by sinking a knife into the white flesh of a large piece, one inch from the edge. Move the knife from side to side until the outer piece separates from the hard shell. Continue until all the meat is removed from the shell.

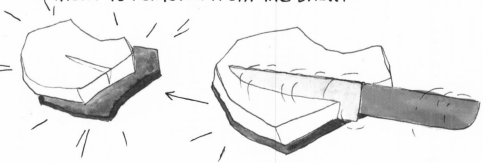

Cut up coconut will last up to one week in the fridge.

How to cut up a mango

1. Hold the mango so that narrow end is pointing up & cut the mango about ¼" from the center of the fruit. You will feel the side of the seed on your knife as you slice through the flesh.

2. Slice the other side in the same way, separating the seed from the two halves of fruit.

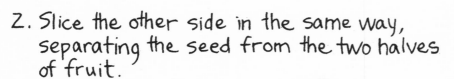

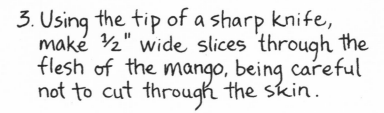

3. Using the tip of a sharp knife, make ½" wide slices through the flesh of the mango, being careful not to cut through the skin.

4. Then make horizontal cuts in the flesh to make cubes.

5. Flip the peel by pulling the sides down & pushing the middle up, the fruit will separate.

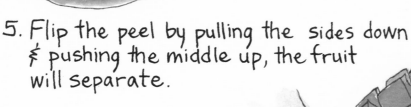

6. With little effort, use your thumbs to separate the flesh from the peel.

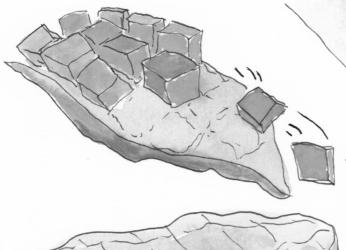

HOW TO CUT UP A WHOLE CHICKEN

A whole bird is usually separated into 8 parts: 2 wings, 2 thighs, 2 drumsticks & 2 breast pieces. If chicken is raw, rinse & pat dry first. Use a sharp knife & give yourself plenty of space by using a large cutting board.

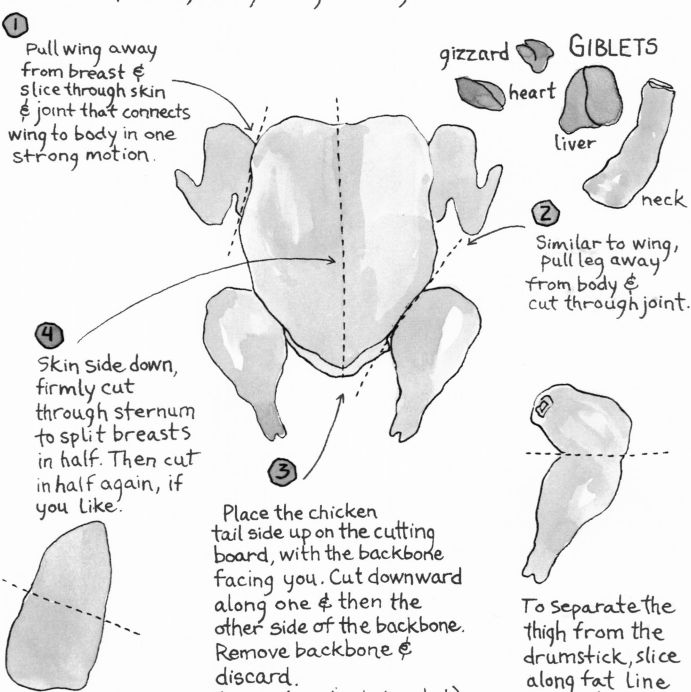

1 Pull wing away from breast & slice through skin & joint that connects wing to body in one strong motion.

GIBLETS
gizzard
heart
liver
neck

2 Similar to wing, pull leg away from body & cut through joint.

4 Skin side down, firmly cut through sternum to split breasts in half. Then cut in half again, if you like.

3 Place the chicken tail side up on the cutting board, with the backbone facing you. Cut downward along one & then the other side of the backbone. Remove backbone & discard.
(or save to make chicken stock)

To separate the thigh from the drumstick, slice along fat line on joint.

An Easy Way to Separate Egg Yolk
Suction! Remove the cap from a clean
plastic soda bottle.
Break an egg into a bowl & place the
bottle just over the surface of the yolk
(yolk must be intact). Squeeze the
bottle & release...! The yolk gets
sucked up in the bottle. Squeeze the
bottle over another bowl, let yolk fall.

Make the most of your garlic

When preparing garlic, smashing each clove with the side of a knife produces a stronger garlic flavor than simply mincing the clove (more of the oils are released). Smash first, then mince, sauté, blend, etc.

When thawing frozen fish

Put ice around the fish & allow it to thaw in the refrigerator slowly, to keep the fish firm. If it changes temperature too quickly, the fish can become mushy.

PALILLOS

PLATOS

METATE

COMAL

Kitchen tools are not what makes food taste good, but having the right ones makes the process more efficient & much more enjoyable.

BATIDORA

COLADORA

PINSZAS

TRASTE

APLASTADOR DE PAPA

CUCHARA de MADERA

LICUADORA

MANDOLINA

TAZAS

BOTELLA

TABLA DE PICAR

CUCHILLOS

BATIDOR

TENEDOR
CUCHARA

MOLCAJETE

CUCHARA para FREÍR

OLLA

ESPÁTULA

My favorite tools in the kitchen

SARTÉN

EXPRIMIDOR

LARD or VEGETABLE SHORTENING?

Whatever your personal feelings about lard, there's no denying it is the authentic choice for most Latin American foods.

Nevertheless, you alone should decide whether to use lard in a recipe or some other fat like butter or vegetable shortening.

Lard is higher in saturated fat & cholesterol than vegetable shortening but lower than butter. In its unsaturated form, lard doesn't contain any trans fatty acids, which are bad for your heart.

Margarine & vegetable shortenings labeled "partially hydrogenated" have trans fats, too. Vegetable oils meanwhile, have a lot less fat & cholesterol than lard & shortening, which makes them more health-conscious choices. But keep in mind that not all vegetable oils are the same in terms of fat, cholesterol & flavor.

Refined Oils: heat processed, often extracted using solvents. Stable under high heat.

Unrefined Oils: cold processed, stronger flavor, more nutrients. Best used under low heat.

Listed in Fahrenheit

SMOKE POINT High

Refined SAFFLOWER OIL	510°
Pomace OLIVE OIL	460°
Refined COCONUT OIL	450°
Refined PEANUT OIL	450°
Refined SESAME OIL	450°
GRAPESEED OIL	420°
Refined CANOLA OIL	400°
Extra Virgin OLIVE OIL	375°
LARD	375°
VEGETABLE SHORTENING	360°
Unrefined BUTTER	350°
Unrefined SOYBEAN OIL	320°
Unrefined SAFFLOWER OIL	225°

SMOKE POINT Low

source: Wikipedia

on FRYING FOOD:

When frying foods, use a cooking oil with a high smoke point. Peanut & canola oil are both excellent choices because they don't break down at high temperatures, which produces an unpleasant taste. Olive oil has a high smoke point, too, but would be a way more expensive choice, especially for frying large amounts.

SAFETY PRECAUTIONS

Remember that hot oil & water should never come in contact, or you risk starting a grease fire. Always keep baking soda & a fire extinguisher nearby & remember to immediately cover the pan with a lid if you see flames!

BEFORE FRYING

Select a heavy, deep pan so oil doesn't spatter all over your kitchen. Make sure that the food you're going to fry is completely dry. Add your food to the pan when the oil starts to sizzle: 350 to 375 degrees F. (177-190 C). Avoid overcrowding the pan. Otherwise, you won't have room to flip your food & the oil won't stay hot enough for frying. If you add too much food at once, the oil will be absorbed by the food instead of searing & crisping it.

AFTERWARDS

Allow the oil to cool down entirely, then pour it into a container with a secure lid. Freezing oil first can make disposal less messy. Never pour oil down the drain! If you like, you can grease your kitchen & garden tools when you're done with it.

Platos
PRINCIPALES
the main dishes

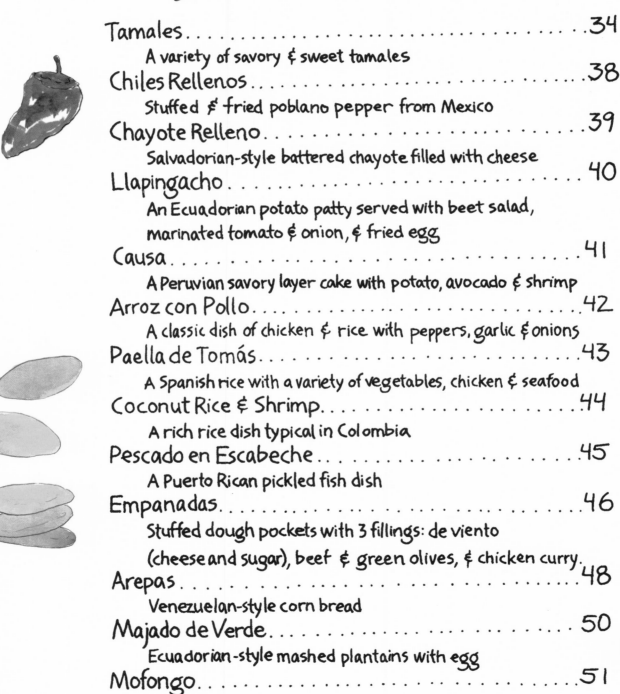

TAMALES

makes about 40 tamales

Yes! This is a large quantity but with so many variations, both sweet & savory, make lots, freeze some & give some away.

The Masa

- 1 16oz package of corn husks OR 40 8"×10" banana leaf pieces
- 2⅔ cups lard OR veggie shortening
- 8 cups (4lbs) fresh, coarse-ground masa.
  If fresh is not available, substitute "masa harina"
- ½ packet active dry yeast
- 1 tbsp salt   • 1 tsp baking powder
- 3½ cups veggie or chicken broth

check your local Latin American Grocery for fresh masa

CORN HUSK TAMALES

Soak the corn husks in water; keep them submerged in water for about 2 hours until soft.

Blot the corn husks dry with a towel before filling them with masa.

The larger the corn husk, the better tamale wrapper it makes, but layering smaller corn husks together into a larger surface works too.

Preparing Tamales:
Add 3tbsp masa to center & press flat. On top of masa, place 2tbsp filling, fold in masa dough, enclosing filling inside. Close corn husk

corn husk tamal

filling inside masa

① ② ③ ④

← Pinch masa in husk when you fold

Mixing the Masa: using an electric mixer, beat the lard or shortening until fluffy.

In a large bowl, mix masa, yeast, salt & baking powder. Slowly add fat to dry ingredients to create a spongy dough. Then add the broth 1 cup at a time until it is the consistency of a paste. I usually divide the dough into thirds: 2/3 for savory & 1/3 for sweet tamales.

The Filling

. . . .

THE SAVORY TAMALE: each kind yields 18 tamales

▷ Chicken & mole (I use premade Doña Maria) OR pasilla salsa OR salsa verde:
- Boil 2 chicken breasts; pull apart meat into strips. Add 2-3 pieces chicken & a spoonful of salsa/mole in the middle of the masa dough.

▷ Chile & queso:
- Heat & peel 3 poblano chiles on stove; cut into "rajas" (strips). Pull apart about 12 oz queso Oaxaca. Fill each tamal with about 2 rajas & 2 pc. queso.

▷ Mixed Veggies of choice:
- Cut up veggies into 1/4" pieces. Sauté with preferred spices until soft. I like sweet potato & bell pepper with cumin.

35

THE SWEET DESSERT TAMALE: yields 12 tamales (⅓ masa recipe)

- 2 cups fresh or frozen fruit (my favorite are berries)
- ¼-½ cup sugar
- 1 tsp lemon juice

Blend all in blender; add water, if needed, for jam-like consistency.

Combine ⅓ portion of masa dough recipe with fruit;
mix; spoon about ¼ cup of fruit masa dough
onto corn husk. Wrap, then steam.
Serve with extra fruit. (optional)

BANANA LEAF TAMALES

Pre-cut banana leaves are available in some Latin
American grocery stores in the refrigerated section.
If fresh banana leaves are available, cut & heat each
on comál to soften before wrapping tamale.
Layer each leaf with aluminum foil, then wrap.

Use chosen fillings
& proportions listed
in corn husk tamales.

Steaming the tamales

1. Use a large stock pot with a metal
   strainer. Fill the pot with water just below strainer.
2. Stack the tamales inside strainer standing on end;
   folded end of tamales should face up. Separate different
   types into sections with a kitchen towel. Pack the top
   with extra corn husks & another
   towel to insulate.

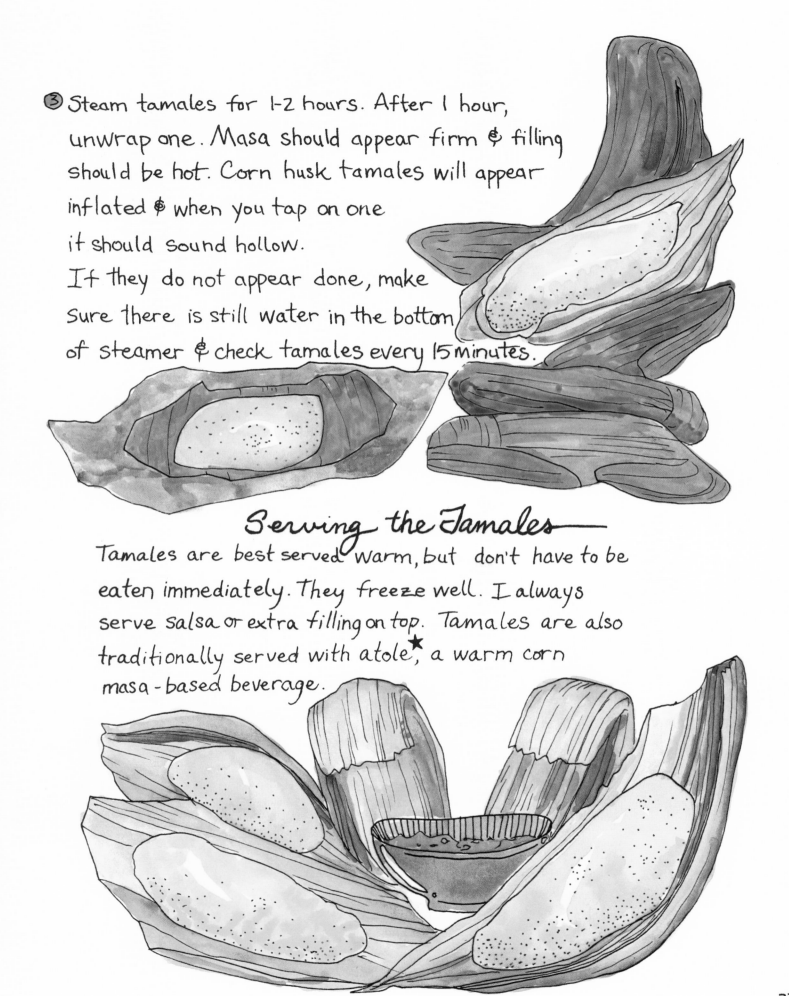

③ Steam tamales for 1-2 hours. After 1 hour, unwrap one. Masa should appear firm & filling should be hot. Corn husk tamales will appear inflated & when you tap on one it should sound hollow.
If they do not appear done, make sure there is still water in the bottom of steamer & check tamales every 15 minutes.

Serving the Tamales

Tamales are best served warm, but don't have to be eaten immediately. They freeze well. I always serve salsa or extra filling on top. Tamales are also traditionally served with atole★, a warm corn masa-based beverage.

CHILES RELLENOS

Serves 6

- 6 poblano chiles
- 12 oz queso Oaxaca
- 5 eggs, separated
- 4 tbsp olive oil
- 2 cups flour & 1 tsp salt, mixed
- 1 cup veggie oil

Blacken the chiles over high heat on comal, rotating so skin blisters all over & they become soft.

Seal chiles in mason jar or plastic bag for 15 min.

Peel skin off chiles then cut small slit.

Using a paring knife, cut out seeds then carefully rinse out loose seeds in sink.

Stuff chile with 2 chunks of cheese the size of your finger.

Close each chile with a toothpick.

Whip the egg whites until peaks form.

Add the yolks & olive oil, mix well.

Cover each chile with a thin layer of flour mixure.

Dip chile in whipped egg. Add thin layer of veggie oil to pan, fry until golden.

Remove toothpicks.

Serve with red cinnamon salsa ★

38

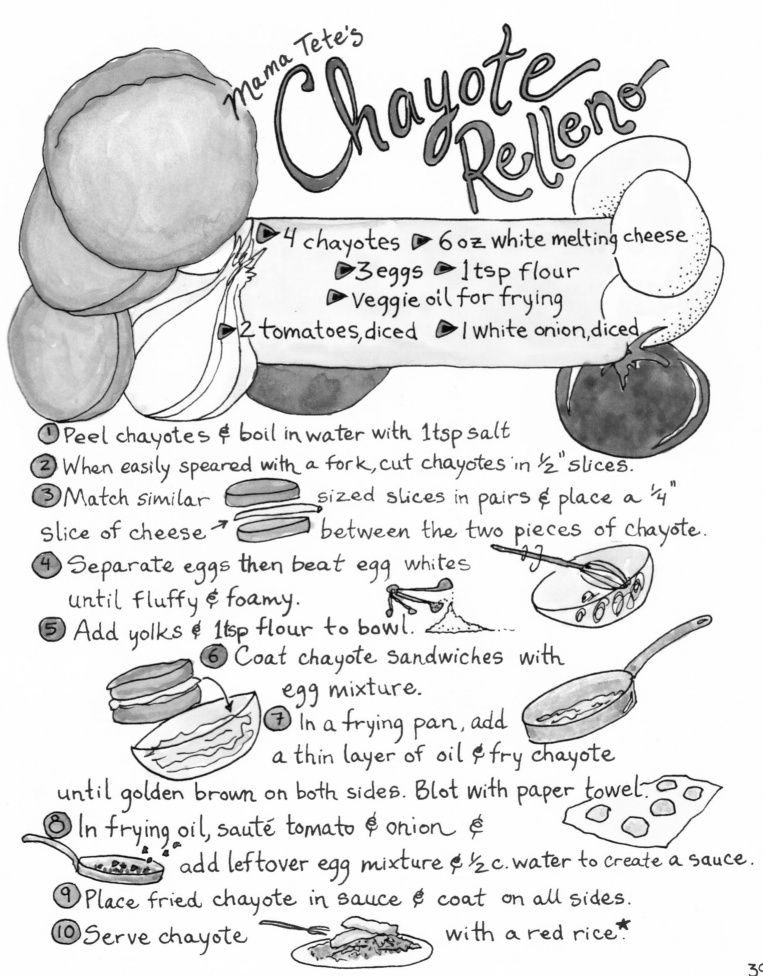

Mama Tete's
Chayote Relleno

- ▶ 4 chayotes ▶ 6 oz white melting cheese
- ▶ 3 eggs ▶ 1 tsp flour
- ▶ Veggie oil for frying
- ▶ 2 tomatoes, diced ▶ 1 white onion, diced

① Peel chayotes & boil in water with 1 tsp salt

② When easily speared with a fork, cut chayotes in ½" slices.

③ Match similar sized slices in pairs & place a ¼" slice of cheese → between the two pieces of chayote.

④ Separate eggs then beat egg whites until fluffy & foamy.

⑤ Add yolks & 1 tsp flour to bowl.

⑥ Coat chayote sandwiches with egg mixture.

⑦ In a frying pan, add a thin layer of oil & fry chayote until golden brown on both sides. Blot with paper towel.

⑧ In frying oil, sauté tomato & onion & add leftover egg mixture & ½ c. water to create a sauce.

⑨ Place fried chayote in sauce & coat on all sides.

⑩ Serve chayote with a red rice*

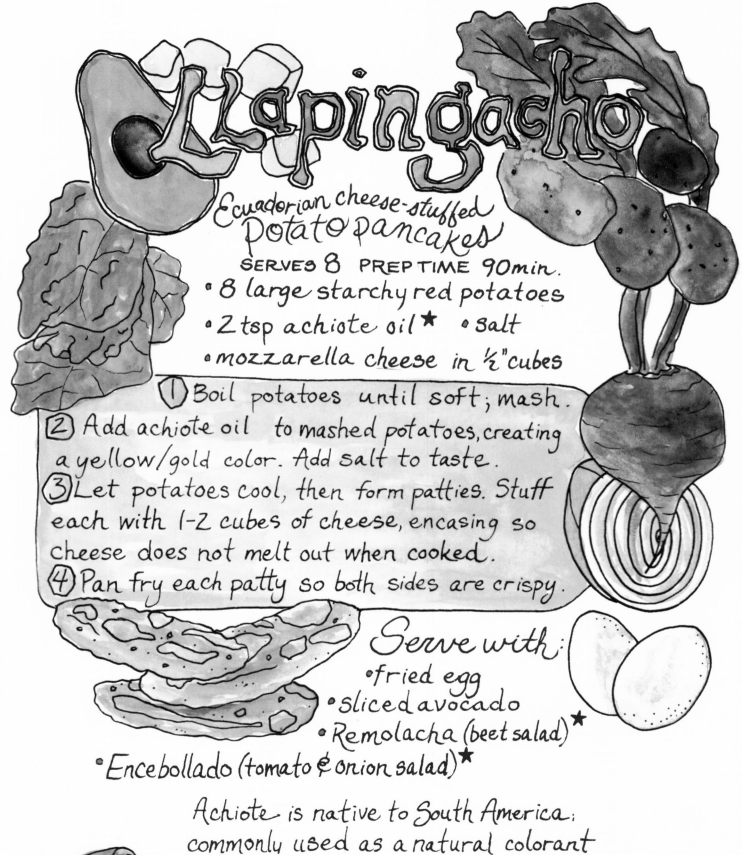

Llapingacho

Ecuadorian cheese-stuffed
Potato Pancakes

SERVES 8   PREP TIME 90min.

- 8 large starchy red potatoes
- 2 tsp achiote oil ★   • salt
- mozzarella cheese in ½" cubes

① Boil potatoes until soft; mash.

② Add achiote oil to mashed potatoes, creating a yellow/gold color. Add salt to taste.

③ Let potatoes cool, then form patties. Stuff each with 1-2 cubes of cheese, encasing so cheese does not melt out when cooked.

④ Pan fry each patty so both sides are crispy.

Serve with:
- fried egg
- sliced avocado
- Remolacha (beet salad) ★
- Encebollado (tomato & onion salad) ★

Achiote is native to South America; commonly used as a natural colorant & has a very mild flavor.

Causa

A peruvian dish of layered potato, shrimp & avocado

The puree & filling of this dish are really versatile. Try replacing the shrimp with chicken & the potato with yam.

The Yellow Mashed Potatoes

- 2 lbs potatoes, peeled
- 2 tbsp salted butter
- 4 tbsp olive oil
- 2 tbsp aji amarillo paste
  If you don't have this here's a pretty good substitute:
  1 roasted, peeled red pepper (jarred ok), ½ tsp turmeric,
  1 tsp olive oil, ¼ tsp Tabasco hot sauce, blend until smooth.
- juice of 1 lime
- 1 tsp salt

1. Boil potatoes, add the butter & mash until smooth. Cool.

2. Add the olive oil, aji amarillo paste (or roasted red pepper paste), lime juice & salt to the potatoes & mix well, refrigerate.

The Filling

- ½ lb raw shrimp, peeled & deveined
- ½ red onion, finely diced
- ½ red bell pepper, finely diced
- ¼ cup olive oil
- 2 tbsp red wine vinegar
- salt

1. Add the shrimp to a saucepan of boiling water & cook until just opaque (about 1 min). Drain & rinse under cold water to stop the cooking process. Refrigerate.

2. Toss together the onion, pepper, olive oil, vinegar & chilled shrimp. Season with salt.

To ASSEMBLE

- 4" deep round mold (A 15 oz aluminum can with both ends cut off works well)
- Olive oil to grease inside of can
- 2 avocados, thinly sliced
- Salt & ground pepper
- Cilantro sprigs (garnish)

1. Lightly oil the inside of the mold & place on a plate. Lightly pack the mold with about 1" of mashed potato, then add a layer of avocado & a dash of salt & pepper then push down gently to fill out the mold. Then add a thin layer of the shrimp filling (so shrimp lay flat) & another ½" layer of the potato.

2. Carefully slide the can off of the causa, using a spoon if necessary to push the layers out of the mold in one piece.

3. Place one shrimp & some of the sauce on top with a couple cilantro leaves to garnish.

4. Serve immediately, otherwise cover, refrigerate & remove the mold right before serving If using the same mold for all causa, be sure to oil the inside before making the next one.

ARROZ con POLLO

serves 6-8
Cooking time: 1.5 hours

- 1 3-5 lb whole chicken
- ¼ cup olive oil
- 1 large white onion, diced
- 2 cloves garlic, smashed
- 1 cup stewed tomatoes
- 5 cups water
- 1 bay leaf

- ½ tsp cumin
- ½ tsp oregano
- ½ tsp turmeric
- 4 cups rice
- 1 cup peas (frozen okay)
- 3 bell peppers, roasted & diced
- 1 can beer (optional)

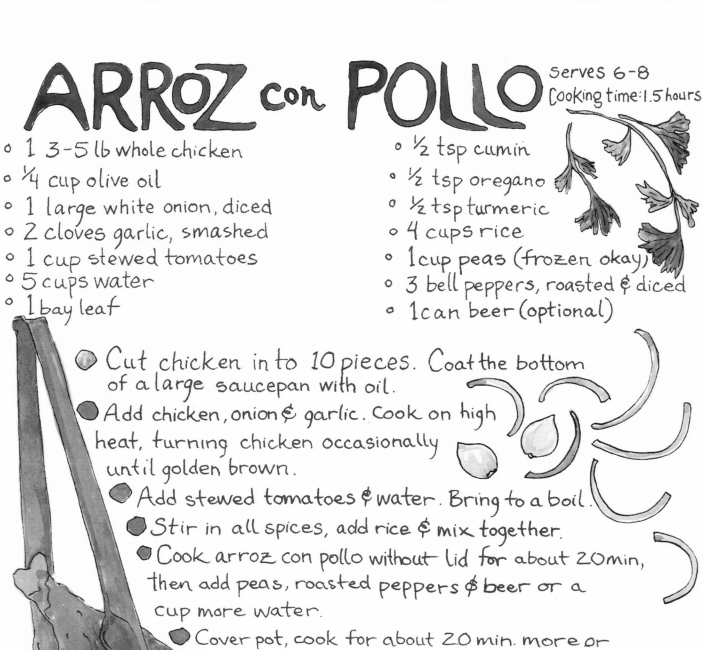

- Cut chicken into 10 pieces. Coat the bottom of a large saucepan with oil.
- Add chicken, onion & garlic. Cook on high heat, turning chicken occasionally until golden brown.
- Add stewed tomatoes & water. Bring to a boil.
- Stir in all spices, add rice & mix together.
- Cook arroz con pollo without lid for about 20 min, then add peas, roasted peppers & beer or a cup more water.
- Cover pot, cook for about 20 min. more or until rice is soft.
- Remove from heat, let stand with lid on for 20 minutes before serving.
- Drizzle with olive oil & season to taste with salt & pepper.

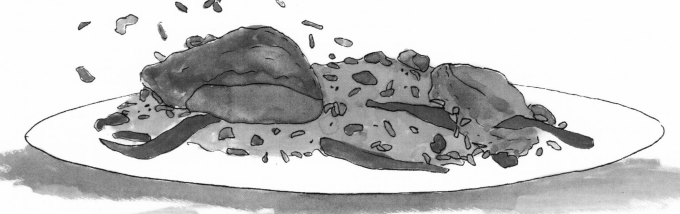

Paella
de Tomás

Serves 8-10
15"-17" paella pan

- Olive oil to cover bottom of pan .... Heat to hot.

- 10 medium sized pieces of chicken ...... Fry, brown both sides.

- 3 onions, chopped .... } Add onions & peppers
- 3 cups bell peppers, sliced .... } sauté until soft (3-5 min)
- 10 garlic cloves, minced .... } then add garlic.

- 2 cups Bomba/Calasparra rice .... Stir, coating rice in oil (5 min).

- 5-6 cups veggie/chicken/seafood broth }
- 40 threads saffron (5 threads p/person) } Cook without stirring paella,
- 4-6 piquillo peppers (from glass jar) sliced } allowing rice to absorb
- 2½ cups fava beans, cooked .... } liquid (10-15 min).
- 3 tomatoes, chopped .... }

- 20 clams, fresh .... } Add on top of paella after
- 20 shrimp, fresh .... } most liquid is absorbed (80%).

- 1 cup green olives........................... Add on top.
- 4 lemons, sliced ....Make available to add when served.

Paella originated in Valencia, Spain, one of the best places for growing Spanish rice: a grain that is more round than most rice & can absorb lots of water while retaining its al dente texture. Best paella is cooked over an open flame & enables a toasted layer to form on the bottom of the pan, called "Socarret," a delicacy to many. Historically, this versatile dish offered cooks the opportunity to use whatever ingredients they had on hand. Regional interpretations emerged & today we enjoy countless variations including vegetarian, seafood & meat medley paella. For a successful paella, one should use the right pan, real saffron & add the ingredients in the proper sequence.

Coconut Rice & Shrimp

6-8 SERVINGS   PREP TIME 1 hour

Popular dish on the coast of Colombia

Shrimp

- 2 lb large shrimp, peeled & deveined
- 3 tbsp olive oil
- ½ tbsp chile powder
- 1 tsp each: salt & pepper

Garnishes

- 3 tbsp fresh parsley, chopped
- 4 limes, quartered

Coconut Rice

- 1 white onion, diced
- 4 cloves garlic, smashed
- 4 tbsp olive oil
- 2 cups rice
- 2 cups coconut milk
- 2 cups chicken broth or water
- 2-3 bay leaves

① Marinate shrimp in olive oil, chile powder, salt & pepper for 20 minutes.

② Sauté diced onion & smashed garlic in 4 tbsp. olive oil in pot.

③ Rinse rice, then add to pot. Stir to coat rice with the oil.

④ Add coconut milk, chicken broth, 1 tsp salt & bay leaves.
Bring to a boil, then reduce heat to low. Simmer for 10 min. with lid on.
Cooking times may vary depending on type of rice used.

⑤ Add marinated shrimp & stir.

⑥ Cover pot with lid for about 15 min. or until all liquid is absorbed & small air holes appear on the surface of the rice.

⑦ Mix parsley into rice & serve with limes.

Use a bowl as a mold:
Press rice in bowl,
place plate on top &
flip. Remove bowl.

Pescado en Escabeche

TRADITIONALLY THIS DISH IS SERVED COLD BUT CAN BE ENJOYED WARM TOO. SERVE WITH MOFONGO FOR A TRUE PUERTO RICAN FEAST!

for the sauce

- 1 cup Olive oil
- ¾ cup distilled white vinegar
- 12 black peppercorns
- 3 bay leaves
- 1 large yellow onion, thinly sliced
- 10 medium carrots, peeled & julienned
- 2-4 cloves garlic, quartered

for the fish

- 2 lbs thick fillets of a firm white fish (cod, tilapia, sea bass)
- 1 large lime
- 2 tsp salt
- ⅓ cup flour
- ¾ cup olive oil
- salad greens of your choice

① In a large pot, mix together all sauce ingredients & simmer on low for 30 min Allow mixture to cool.

② Rinse fish then pat dry. Squeeze lime juice over the fish fillets & sprinkle with 2 tsp salt all over. Dredge the fish in flour, lightly covering all sides.

③ In a frying pan, heat ¾ cup olive oil. Add fish slices to pan & cook on medium heat until the fish is golden brown on both sides (5-6 min first side, 3-4 on the other.) Reduce the heat to low & cook the fish fillets for 5-10 min. or until fish flakes easily when tested with a fork.

④ In a deep glass dish, arrange alternate layers of sauce & fish beginning & finishing with the sauce.

⑤ Cover & refrigerate for up to 24 hours before serving, this will improve the pickled flavor.
To serve, arrange the fish on a bed of greens (discard bay leaves) & spoon some of the sauce over the fish.

EMPANADAS

yields 14

One of the many portable stuffed dough pockets of the world. Found throughout Latin America in various sizes & are sometimes referred to as pasteles.

The Dough

- 2 cups white flour, sifted
- 2 tsp baking powder
- ½ tsp salt
- ⅔ cup veggie shortening/lard
- ¼ cup sugar dissolved in ½ cup milk
- ½ tsp achiote oil. ✱

This 'hot pocket' could be categorized with the Indian samosa, Italian calzone, Afghani bolani, Indonesian pastel & the Jamaican patty.

Sift all dry ingredients together & cut shortening into little bits. Add the sweetened milk & achiote oil a little at a time, kneading with your hands. The dough should resemble pie dough. Roll the dough ⅛" thick then cut into 4"-5" circles. Press a 5" lid in the dough to cut the circle. Chill the dough rounds for 20 min.

FORMING THE EMPANADAS

1. Place about 2-3 tbsp of filling of choice in center 2. fold in half
3. Pinch around edges to make sure the filling stays inside.

4. Form the scalloped edge by pulling & folding the edge over. In Spanish these are "repulgos de la empanada". Bake or Fry.

To Bake:
Preheat oven to 375°; brush each with egg white then place on greased pan & bake for 15 minutes or until golden brown.

To Fry:
Fill saucepan with about ½" veggie oil, heat to 375° & fry each until golden brown, about a minute on each side.

Empanadas de Viento *de Ecuador*

Soft, sweet & airy appearing only to be filled with wind

- 2½ cups grated melting cheese (quesillo, queso Oaxaca)
- ½ cup granulated sugar   • 2 cups frying oil

After preparing the dough, add 2 tbsp cheese to each. Deep fry, then sprinkle a little sugar on top before it cools. This allows sugar to stick. Immediately serve. Typically enjoyed alongside warm morocho. ★

Shredded Beef with green olives

- 3 tbsp olive oil
- 1 large onion, diced
- 1 large red pepper, cored & diced
- 1 tomato, diced
- 2 tsp balsamic vinegar
- 1 cup shredded cooked beef
- ½ cup finely chopped cilantro
- ¼ cup green olives, pitted & chopped

Heat the olive oil in a large pan over med-high heat, then add the onion, pepper, tomato & vinegar & sauté until vegetables are soft. Add the shredded beef, cilantro & olives & simmer for another 5 minutes. Season to taste with salt & pepper. Spoon 1-3 tbsp of mixture into empanadas, depending on the size.

Chicken Curry for empanadas

- ½ white onion, diced
- 2 chicken breasts, sliced
- 1½ tsp yellow curry
- salt & pepper to taste
- ½ cup sour cream
- ¼ cup golden raisins

In large pan sauté onions. Season chicken with 1 tsp curry, salt & pepper then add to pan & cook. Stir in sour cream, the rest of the curry & raisins. Lower heat & simmer for 10-20 minutes.
Add a couple spoonfuls to fill each empanada

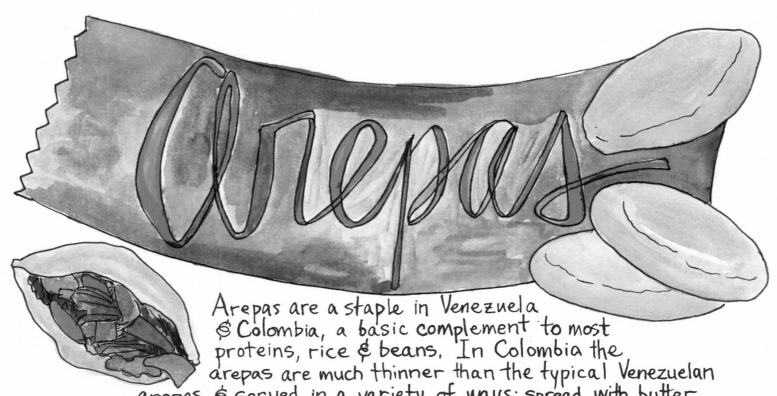

Arepas

Arepas are a staple in Venezuela & Colombia, a basic complement to most proteins, rice & beans. In Colombia the arepas are much thinner than the typical Venezuelan arepas, & served in a variety of ways: spread with butter on top, served with fresh cheese, or split open & served with hogao (a stewed tomato salsa). In Venezuela, it's common to scoop out the doughy inside of the arepa then fill the shell with savory combinations of shredded meat, vegetables & beans.

My friend Luz taught me her family recipe: in typical Venezuelan style, the arepas are puffy & thick & when eating them we scooped out the soft, doughy inside & mixed it with queso crema & ate it on the side of our arepas, which we stuffed full of caraotas (stewed black beans), pollo desmenchado (shredded chicken) platanitos fritos (fried ripe plantains) & mojo sauce.

LA MASA: MASAREPA

arepas ↓

Unlike Mexican-style tortillas, arepas are made from a precooked, ground corn flour that does not go through the process of nixtamalization. There are a handful of masarepa flours on the market including Harina PAN (a white & yellow variety) which is by far the most popular variety, known for its smooth consistency.

← Tamales, tortillas

AREPAS Venezolanas

Makes 10-12 arepas

ingredients

- 2 cups yellow Harina PAN
- 2 cups white Harina PAN
    - or 4 cups of the mixed type
- 2 tsp. salt
- 3 ¼ cups warm water
- 1 tbsp. olive oil
- For griddle: olive oil or butter as needed to grease surface.

Mix together the white & yellow harina & salt in a large bowl. Add 2½ cups of warm water & mix with your hands. Then slowly add the remaining water. The dough should be sticky but smooth & not containing any lumps. Add a bit more corn or water until this texture is achieved.

Let stand for at least 10 minutes, uncovered. Mixture will firm up & you should be able to form a ball.

Heat griddle over medium heat & add 1 tbsp olive oil to cover surface. Pinch off some of the dough & roll into a 2" ball, then flatten between your palms to make a 4" disk. Wet your palms before forming each ball to keep the dough from sticking to your hands.

Working in batches, cook on the hot, well-greased griddle, turning once, until golden brown & crispy outside (10-15 min.)

Keep prepared arepas warm in a 275° oven until ready to serve.

Eat with desired toppings, including but not limited to shredded meat, queso telita (queso Oaxaca), beans, mojo sauce,* sliced tomato & queso crema.

MAJADO DE VERDE

an Ecuadorian breakfast food

SERVES 4

- 4 green plantains, peeled & cut in 1" chunks.
- 1 white onion, diced
- ½ tsp achiote oil ★
- 4 eggs, beaten
- 1 handful queso fresco, crumbled
- 2 sliced avocados
- Ecuadorian ají or ají criollo ★

1. Boil plantains in water for 30 minutes or until soft.
2. Mash the plantains with a potato masher, keep some small chunks.
3. Sauté onion in oil until soft.
4. Add plantains & beaten eggs, salt to taste. Cook (10 min)
5. Serve immediately with queso fresco, avocado & ají.

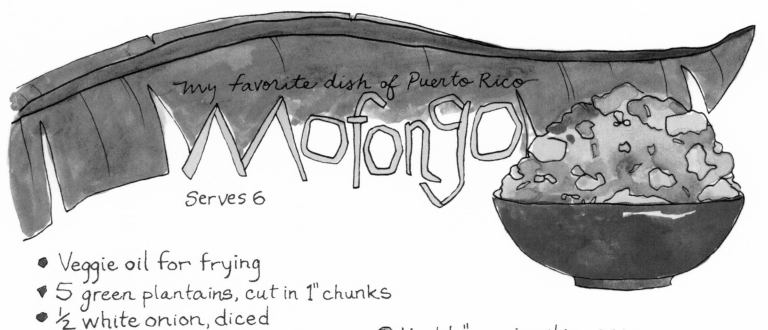

my favorite dish of Puerto Rico

Mofongo

Serves 6

- Veggie oil for frying
- 5 green plantains, cut in 1" chunks
- ½ white onion, diced
- 2-4 cloves garlic, smashed
- 1-2 cups chopped cooked chicken
  (I use leftovers from roast chicken)
- 1 tsp salt
- 4 cups chicken
  or veggie stock, warm
- 1 tsp achiote oil *

① Heat ½" veggie oil in a pan.

② Fry plantains until golden brown.

③ In another pan, sauté onion & garlic in veggie oil (2 min), add chicken & salt

④ Combine plantains with 2 cups broth & achiote oil in food processor. Pulse but keep chunky. Transfer to bowl.

⑤ Add onion/garlic/chicken to bowl, stir. Pour a little broth over each portion when serving.

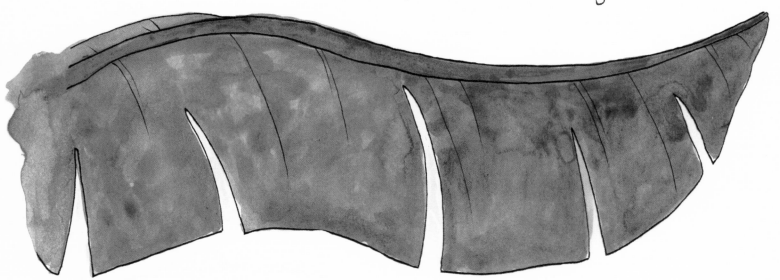

Variation: substitute shrimp for chicken to make a "camarónfongo".

fish tacos

6 servings

- 1lb firm white fish (cod, mahi mahi, tilapia) as fresh as possible

The Marinade { ¼ cup lime juice, ¼ cup veggie oil
1 pinch coriander, cumin, salt & ground chile

- fresh corn tortillas

The Salsa stir together!
{ ½ cup mayo, ½ cup sour cream
½ tsp minced capers, ¼ cup lime
1 pinch coriander, cumin, ground chile
½ handful chopped cilantro, salt to taste }

1. Mix marinade & brush all over fish. Marinate for 20min.
2. Fry fish in veggie oil over med-high heat, flipping when bottom side is opaque. Add more oil if needed. Second side will take less time to cook (around 2 minutes). Salt & pepper to taste.
3. Let fish rest for 5 minutes, then flake with a fork
4. Warm corn tortillas on stove.
5. Place 2-3 chunks of fish in each tortilla, drizzle with the salsa & top with some cabbage coleslaw.★
6. Serve fish tacos right after assembling, with sliced lime & cilantro leaves on the side.

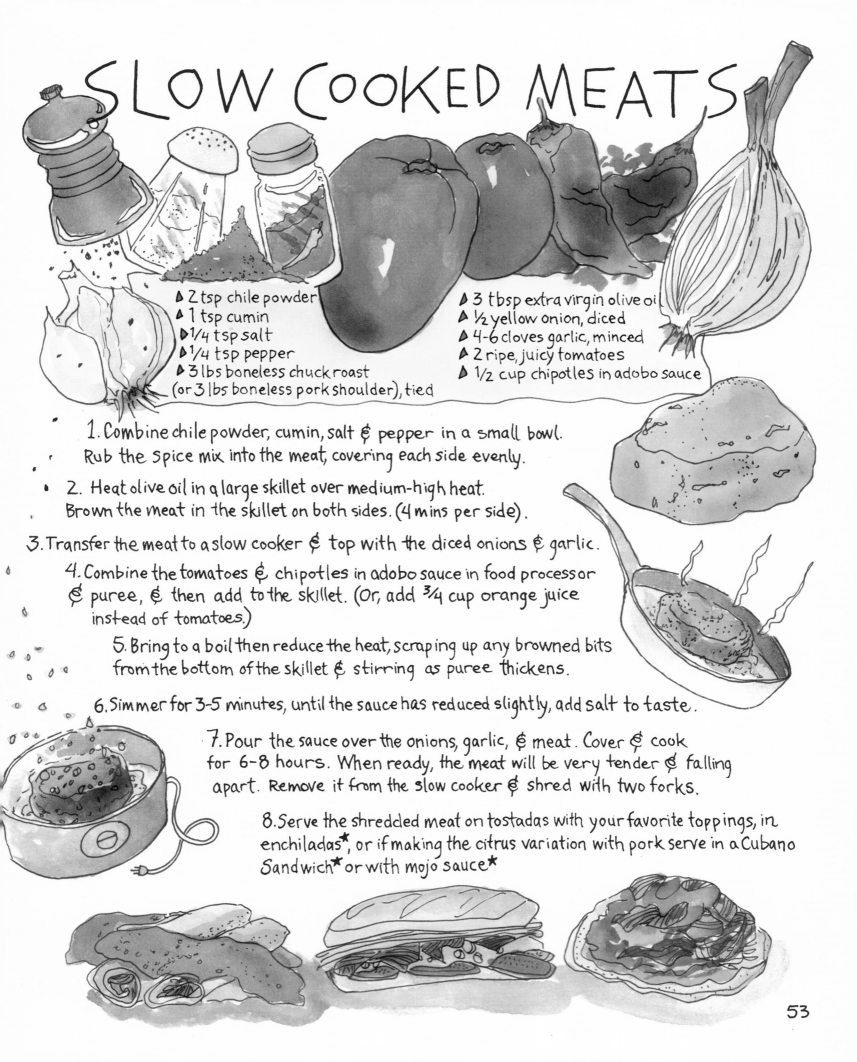

SLOW COOKED MEATS

- 2 tsp chile powder
- 1 tsp cumin
- 1/4 tsp salt
- 1/4 tsp pepper
- 3 lbs boneless chuck roast (or 3 lbs boneless pork shoulder), tied

- 3 tbsp extra virgin olive oil
- 1/2 yellow onion, diced
- 4-6 cloves garlic, minced
- 2 ripe, juicy tomatoes
- 1/2 cup chipotles in adobo sauce

1. Combine chile powder, cumin, salt & pepper in a small bowl. Rub the spice mix into the meat, covering each side evenly.

2. Heat olive oil in a large skillet over medium-high heat. Brown the meat in the skillet on both sides. (4 mins per side).

3. Transfer the meat to a slow cooker & top with the diced onions & garlic.

4. Combine the tomatoes & chipotles in adobo sauce in food processor & puree, & then add to the skillet. (Or, add 3/4 cup orange juice instead of tomatoes.)

5. Bring to a boil then reduce the heat, scraping up any browned bits from the bottom of the skillet & stirring as puree thickens.

6. Simmer for 3-5 minutes, until the sauce has reduced slightly, add salt to taste.

7. Pour the sauce over the onions, garlic, & meat. Cover & cook for 6-8 hours. When ready, the meat will be very tender & falling apart. Remove it from the slow cooker & shred with two forks.

8. Serve the shredded meat on tostadas with your favorite toppings, in enchiladas*, or if making the citrus variation with pork serve in a Cubano Sandwich* or with mojo sauce*

Chicken Tinga

SHREDDED CHICKEN IN RICH, SWEET, TOMATO-CHILE SAUCE

◄◄· serves 6 ·►►

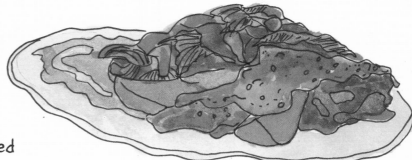

INGREDIENTS:

- 6 Roma tomatoes
- 2 tomatillos, husked & rinsed
- 4 tbsp olive oil
- 2½ lb skin-on, bone-in chicken thighs (4-6 pieces)
- Salt & ground pepper
- 1 medium onion, diced
- 3 garlic cloves, minced
- ¼ cup chipotle adobo sauce*
- ½ tsp dried oregano, or 1 sprig fresh
- ½ tsp dried thyme, or 1 sprig fresh

SERVE WITH:

- Salsa verde*
- 1 cup cilantro, chopped
- 1 avocado, sliced
- Fresh tortillas

1. In pot, cover tomatoes & tomatillos with water. Boil until soft, about 10 minutes. Place in blender with ¼ cup water from pot & process until smooth.

2. Heat 2 tbsp olive oil in a pan over medium heat. Season chicken with salt & pepper & pan-fry chicken, flipping after 15 minutes to brown on both sides. Cook until juices run clear when pierced with a knife, 25-30 minutes. Transfer to a plate. When cool, shred chicken by hand, removing bones & large pieces of fat.

3. Scrape the chicken fat & any browned bits from the bottom of the pan, but leave in to add flavor. Add the remaining 2 tbsp olive oil & heat over medium heat. Add onions and sauté until translucent. Then add minced garlic, reserved tomato/tomatillo puree. Add ¼ cup chipotle adobo sauce*, the oregano, thyme, 1 tsp salt & 1 tsp pepper. Simmer, stirring occasionally, as mixture thickens, about 10 minutes. (If you used fresh herbs, remove the thyme & oregano sprigs.)

4. Add the shredded chicken to sauce, continue to stir as chicken integrates with the sauce & soaks up some of the liquid, 1-3 minutes.

5. Serve over warm tortillas with salsa verde* chopped cilantro & avocado as accompaniments.

el CUBANO:

THE CUBAN SANDWICH

Makes 4 large sandwiches.

☑ 1 loaf bread: The authentic bread is called pan de agua. It's long like a baguette but not as crusty. A white sandwich roll like a Mexican bolillo or a baguette with a thinner crust can be substituted.

Variation: prepare another Cuban Classic Sandwich, La Medianoche, by switching up the bread: serve the same ingredients pressed inside a sweet egg bread, like Challah.

☑ ¼ cup butter, softened
☑ 4 dill pickles, sliced
☑ ½ lb pulled pork
☑ 4 tbsp mojo sauce*
☑ ½ lb ham, sliced
☑ ½ lb mild swiss cheese, sliced
☑ yellow mustard (optional)

One of the most delicious ways to eat ham, cheese & bread, originating in Cuba but perfected in Miami & Tampa, Florida.

① Cut the bread into sandwich lengths (6"-8"). Then cut each in half and spread the 2 tbsp butter evenly on the inside of both halves.

② Assemble each sandwich in this order:

1 sliced pickle, a quarter of the pulled pork, mojo sauce, a quarter of the ham, Swiss cheese & mustard.

I've had Cuban sandwiches with either just mojo sauce or yellow mustard but neither is required, & having both together in the same sandwich is perfectly acceptable & delicious!

③ Add 1 tsp butter to a hot griddle or pan, then arrange the Cubano sandwiches on the hot surface.

④ Flatten the sandwiches using a heavy skillet or foil-wrapped brick if you don't have a sandwich press. Pressing the sandwich to about ½ the original size is key – the bread toasts while the cheese melts & all the juices blend together.

⑤ Grill the sandwiches on medium heat for two to three minutes on each side until bread is golden brown.

⑥ Cut the sandwiches in half & serve hot or cold with yellow mustard on the side.

55

Enchiladas Verdes

serves 4-6

- 6 anaheim chiles
- 6 tomatillos
- ½ cup cream or queso crema (optional)
- salt to taste
- 10-15 corn tortillas
- ½ cup canola oil to fry
- 1 lb skinless chicken breast, cooked
- 1 cup queso fresco, crumbled
- 3 garlic cloves
- 1 white onion

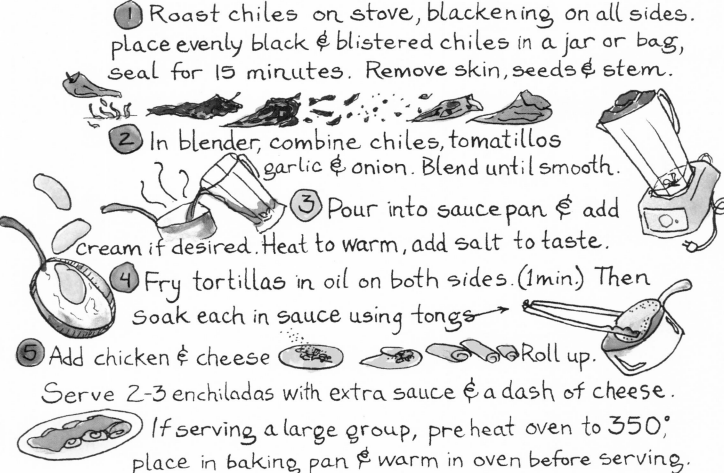

1 Roast chiles on stove, blackening on all sides. place evenly black & blistered chiles in a jar or bag, seal for 15 minutes. Remove skin, seeds & stem.

2 In blender, combine chiles, tomatillos garlic & onion. Blend until smooth.

3 Pour into sauce pan & add cream if desired. Heat to warm, add salt to taste.

4 Fry tortillas in oil on both sides. (1min.) Then soak each in sauce using tongs →

5 Add chicken & cheese ⬤ Roll up.

Serve 2-3 enchiladas with extra sauce & a dash of cheese.

If serving a large group, preheat oven to 350°, place in baking pan & warm in oven before serving.

Enchiladas Rojas
DE PAPA Y ZANAHORIA

Sauce Ingredients

4 lbs ripe whole tomatoes
1 lb whole yellow onion, peeled
1 jalapeño, cut lengthwise
6 garlic cloves, unpeeled
3/4 tsp salt, or to taste
3 tbsp tomato paste

Enchiladas Ingredients

1.5 lbs potatoes
1 lb carrots
1 tbsp Olive Oil
salt
queso cotija, crumbled
corn tortillas (30)

Toppings Ingredients

2 lbs shredded beef or
      shredded pork *
1/2 cup queso crema
1/2 cup queso cotija, crumbled
1/3 cup green onions, chopped
2 ripe avocados, scooped & sliced
1/2 small green cabbage, shredded
fresh lime wedges

SERVES 10-12. MAKES 20-25 ENCHILADAS

The Sauce

- Line a large skillet with a sheet of aluminum foil & heat on high.
- Roast the tomatoes & onions on the foil turning until the skin is partially blackened, then remove from pan.
- Add the jalapeño & garlic & roast until they are soft.
- Peel the garlic & process with all other sauce ingredients in blender or food processor.
- Transfer sauce to saucepan & heat on medium, add more salt to taste, set aside 1/2 cup of the sauce to use with potato & carrot filling.

The Filling

- Peel potatoes & carrots, boil until they are almost tender but still firm. Drain, cool & dice into 1/2" cubes.
- Heat 1 tbsp olive oil in a large pan, add the potatoes & carrots & lightly fry them (5 min) then add 1/2 cup of the red sauce.
- Add salt to taste & 3-4 tbsp cotija cheese, then stir & lower the heat.
- In a large sauté pan, cover bottom of pan with oil, about 1/4" deep, heat on medium until oil is hot.
- Carefully add one tortilla to the pan, covering it with oil and heating it up so that it softens & becomes slick, turning once to lightly fry both sides (5 seconds).
- Then dip the warm tortilla in the red sauce and immediately fill with 1-2 tbsp of the potato/carrot filling & fold over once to close enchilada. Place on serving plate.
- You can serve enchiladas on a large platter or as individual servings (2-3 per person).
- After enchiladas are filled, add a generous portion of the shredded meat on top of each serving. Cover the meat with the remaining red sauce and add desired toppings on top of enchilada.
- Optional: serve with a red or green rice on the side.

LOMO SALTADO
Peruvian Beef & Potato Stir Fry
Serves 6

- 5 tbsp extra virgin olive oil
- 1 tsp cumin
- Salt & ground pepper
- 1 lb beef tenderloin, thinly sliced into 4" pieces. (Variation: 1 lb boneless chicken breast, sliced)
- 1½ cups vegetable oil, for frying
- ¾ lb russet potatoes, julienned & soaked in ice water for at least 1 hour. OR ¾ lb frozen French fries.
- 1 red onion, sliced
- 2 tbsp chopped Ají Amarillo (Peruvian pepper). If you can't find ají amarillo, pickled jalapeños are an inauthentic but tasty substitute.
- 3 tbsp soy sauce
- 3 tbsp balsamic vinegar
- 2 cloves garlic, minced
- 4 roma tomatoes, sliced
- ½ cup chopped cilantro
- White rice, on the side
- ají criollo*

1. Combine 4 tbsp olive oil, cumin, & a generous pinch of salt & pepper in a bowl, stir in beef & marinate (20 min).

2. In a wok, heat 1" of vegetable oil. Add the potatoes & fry over high heat until golden & crisp (6-8 min.) Remove with a slotted spoon & drain on paper towels. Let oil in wok cool, then transfer to a container for reuse.

3. Heat the remaining 1 tbsp olive oil in the wok, add the beef, onions & ají amarillo & stir fry over high heat until browned.

4. Stir in soy sauce, vinegar & garlic & cook (1 min). Add the tomato & cook until slightly softened (about 1 min)

5. Toss in the French fries last so they get covered in sauce but remain somewhat crisp. Mix in the cilantro. Serve right away with rice & ají criollo*.

Encebollado

FISH SOUP with YUCA

~ Typical in coastal Ecuador & N. Peru ~

The Soup
- ½ yellow onion
- 2 large tomatoes
- 3 tbsp olive oil
- 2 tsp ground cumin
- 1 tsp chile powder
- 10 cups water
- ½ cup chopped cilantro
- 2 lbs fresh tuna, swordfish or firm white fish like cod.
- 1 lb yuca, peeled
- Salt & pepper to taste

The toppings
- Popcorn
- Aji ★
- Marinated tomato, lime, onion ★
- Chulpe ★

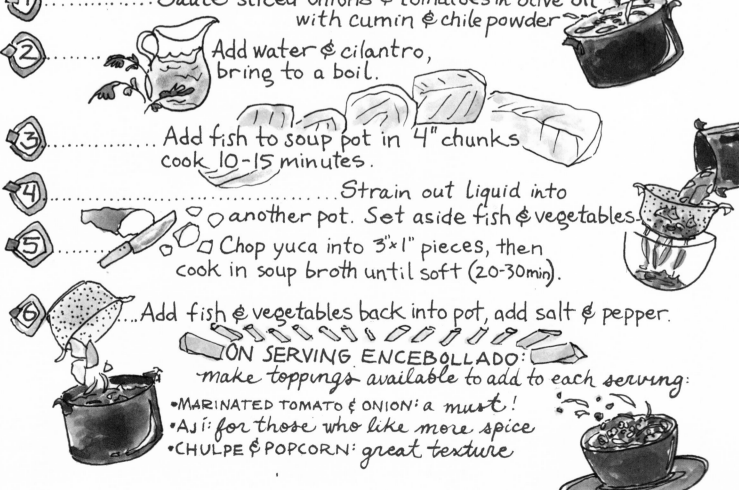

1. .... Sauté sliced onions & tomatoes in olive oil with cumin & chile powder

2. .... Add water & cilantro, bring to a boil.

3. .... Add fish to soup pot in 4" chunks cook 10-15 minutes.

4. .... Strain out liquid into another pot. Set aside fish & vegetables.

5. .... Chop yuca into 3"×1" pieces, then cook in soup broth until soft (20-30min).

6. ...Add fish & vegetables back into pot, add salt & pepper.

ON SERVING ENCEBOLLADO: make toppings available to add to each serving:

- MARINATED TOMATO & ONION: a must!
- AJI: for those who like more spice
- CHULPE & POPCORN: great texture

Gazpacho

a cold soup to sip

Serves 6, prep time 20 min

- 6-7 large tomatoes
- 1 large cucumber
- ½ sweet onion
- 2 cloves garlic
- 3 tbsp olive oil
- 3 tbsp red wine vinegar
- 1 tbsp pepper
- 2 tsp salt
- 1½ cups ice water (optional)

Cut tomatoes in wedges, blend with cucumber, onion & garlic.
Add oil, vinegar, pepper & salt.
Blend, then add water & mix in bowl or pitcher, chill.

Serve gazpacho with garnishes:
Chopped tomatoes, onions, cucumbers, bell peppers

POSOLE

Serves 12-15

This is a recipe for posole rojo con pollo. Many Mexicans serve this for holidays, which is why it is always made in a big quantity to feed lots of people. "Posole" actually refers to hominy, the large kernel corn that is in the soup with meat & meat broth. The soup itself is very simple; what makes it great are the garnishes added upon serving.

The Soup

- 6-8 guajillo chiles
- 3-4 tbsp oil
- 1 cup water
- 6 cloves garlic
- 1 white onion, chopped
- 3 lbs boneless chicken
- 3 bay leaves
- 2 tbsp dried oregano
- 4 cups chicken broth
- 3 × 15 oz cans hominy, drained

1. In medium-size saucepan, heat 6-8 guajillo chiles with 3-4 tbsp oil. When soft, add 1 cup water & heat with garlic & onion (10 min). Purée in blender.

2. Pour through strainer into large soup pot. Discard residue.

3. Slice chicken into strips & add to pot with bay leaves, oregano chicken broth & hominy.

4. Simmer for 1 hour. Salt to taste.

The Garnishes

serve on big platters in center of table for all.

- green onion, chopped
- 5 limes, quartered
- 1 bunch radishes, sliced
- 2 avocados diced
- ½ small cabbage, thinly sliced

La Sopa Azteca

Serves 6-8, prep time 40 min

- 20 corn tortillas
- 1 cup frying oil

- 6 roma tomatoes
- 3 garlic cloves
- 1 white onion
- 4 cups chicken broth
- 2 chicken breasts, cooked
- 1 can diced green chiles
- 1 bunch epazote
- Salt & Pepper to taste
- 4 avocados

- Cut the corn tortillas into 1" squares. Fry tortilla chips in oil in pan until golden brown.
- Boil tomatoes in pot of water for 5 minutes, drain.
- Combine boiled tomato, garlic & onion in blender; blend until smooth.
- Transfer blender contents to soup pot; add 4 cups broth, simmer (15 minutes).
- Cut chicken breast into strips, add to soup with green chile & leaves of epazote, then season with salt & pepper. Simmer for 5 minutes.

Serve with sliced avocado & fresh tortilla chips, which can be mixed in each bowl when served.

Locro de papa

A Classic Ecuadorian Potato Soup

serves 8-10

Ingredients

- 1 lb pork belly, cut into bite-sized cubes
- 2 tbsp Achiote Oil*
- 1 tbsp Butter
- 4 bunches scallions, green & white parts separated & minced
- 4 lbs starchy potatoes, peeled & diced
- 8 cups water
- 4 cups Milk
- 10 whole cilantro stems
- 1 whole fresh rocoto chile
- 2 tsp salt
- 1 tsp ground coriander
- ½ tsp pepper
- ½ tsp cumin

Garnishes:

- 3 avocados, pitted, peeled & sliced
- 1 cup grated mozzarella cheese
- aji criollo*
- fried scallion greens
- crispy pork belly

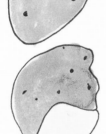

1. Heat the broiler. Arrange the pork belly pieces on a pan & broil until crisp. Transfer to a paper towel-lined plate to cool. Set aside 2 tbsp pork fat for the soup.
2. Heat the achiote oil, the reserved pork fat (or olive oil) and butter in a large soup pot over medium heat.
3. Add the minced scallion whites & cook until translucent.
4. Add the potatoes & fry for 5 minutes, stirring occasionally, then add the water & bring to a boil.
5. Reduce the heat to medium-low & add the milk, cilantro stems, rocoto chile, salt, coriander, pepper & cumin. Simmer, stirring occasionally, until potatoes are soft.
6. Puree the soup. Let soup rest for 10 minutes before serving.
7. While the soup rests, fry the scallion greens in 1 tbsp olive oil until crisp. Garnishes are traditionally added on top of each dish in the kitchen just before serving but a fun alternative is to allow each person to add their own garnishes at the table. A method I learned from my Ecuadorian friends, chefs Sebastian & Pedro, is to serve the soup in a large pitcher so that each guest can serve himself by first filling a bowl with grated cheese, then pouring in the soup & adding the desired garnishes.

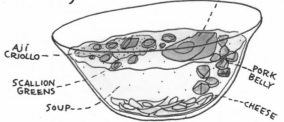

LOCRO DE ZAPALLO (PUMPKIN)

A variation of locro, a potato-based soup from the Andean region.

Serves 6

- 1 onion
- 3 cloves garlic
- 2 tbsp olive oil
- 6 cups chicken/veggie broth
- 1 lb fresh pumpkin, peeled & cut in 1" cubes

- ½ lb small waxy potatoes (I like fingerlings)
- ½ tsp achiote oil*
- ½ tsp cumin
- salt & pepper to taste
- ¼ cup cotija cheese
- fresh oregano

▸ Sauté onions & garlic in oil & add to blender with 1 cup chicken broth. Blend.
▸ Heat onion/garlic & 5 cups broth over medium-high heat; add raw pumpkin & cook for 20 min.
▸ Add small potatoes (cut in half if needed).
▸ Simmer for another 20 min. or until both pumpkin & potatoes are soft, add achiote.
▸ Season with cumin, salt & pepper
▸ Garnish with a bit of cotija cheese & oregano

¡Pepitas! Roasted Pumpkin Seeds

Bonus Snack

- 1 cup raw, washed pumpkin seeds
- 1-2 tbsp olive oil
- salt

optional: ½ tsp ground chile juice from ½ lime

- Preheat oven to 375°
- Mix seeds with oil & seasonings
- Spread on a baking sheet, roast in oven for 15-20 minutes.
- Stir seeds half way through to evenly cook. Seeds will appear golden & puffy when finished roasting.

SANCOCHO de GALLINA

A HEARTY, COLOMBIAN-STYLE STEW WITH YUCA, CORN, CHICKEN & MORE

serves 8

- □ 3 tbsp achiote oil *
- □ 1 medium onion
- □ 2 roma tomatoes, chopped
- □ 4 garlic cloves, minced
- □ 1 tsp cumin
- □ salt & pepper to taste
- □ 1 whole chicken, cut in 10 pieces
- □ 10-12 cups water
- □ 2 carrots, peeled & sliced

- □ ½ lb potatoes, peeled & chopped
- □ 1 green plantain
- □ 1 large yuca, peeled & chopped (3 cups)
- tied in cheesecloth { 2 sprigs fresh thyme / 1 dried bay leaf / 1-2 tsp chopped fresh parsley
- □ 2-3 ears of corn cut in 2" pieces
- □ 1-2 avocados, sliced
- □ aji criollo *

① Heat achiote oil in a 12-quart pot over medium heat, add onions & cook until soft, 5-10 min, then stir in tomatoes, garlic & cumin. Add ½ tsp salt.

② Add chicken & 10 cups water & bring to a boil, then reduce heat & simmer for 15 minutes. Skim off the froth that rises to the top & discard.

③ Add carrots, potatoes, plantain, yuca & herbs tied in cheesecloth to pot, stir. Add 1-2 cups more water if the soup looks dry. Bring back to a boil then reduce heat to med-low & add the corn. Continue to cook sancocho, covered, for 20 more minutes. Add salt & pepper to taste.

④ Serve sancocho in bowls with sliced avocado & aji criollo* on the side, to add as desired.

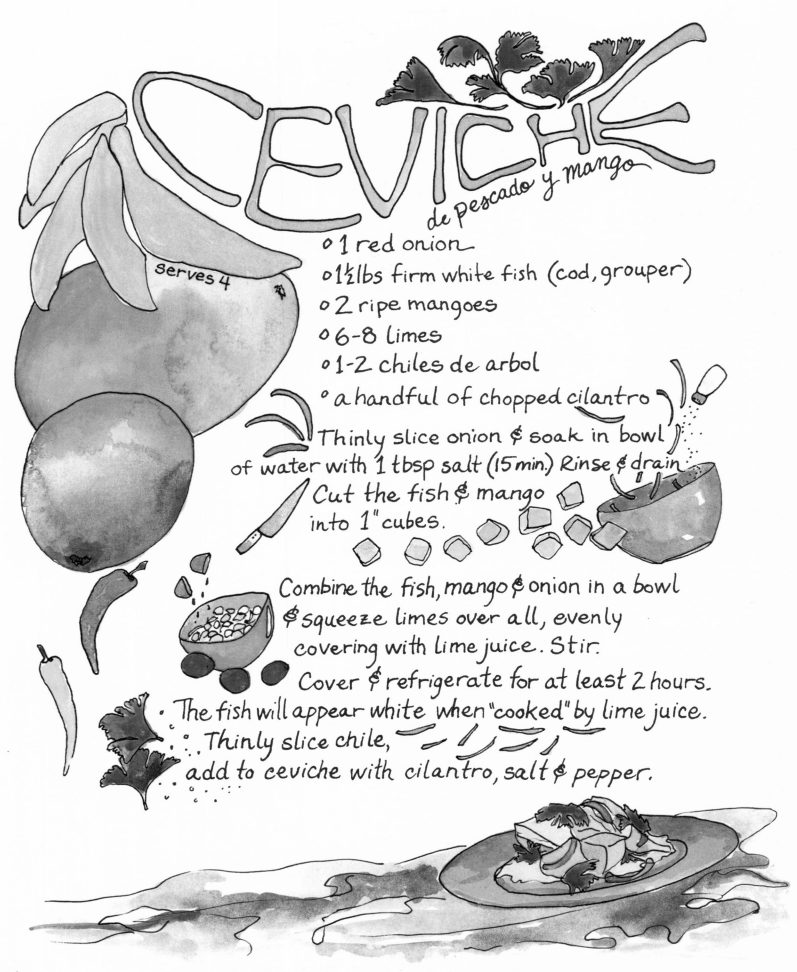

CEVICHE
de pescado y mango

serves 4

- 1 red onion
- 1½ lbs firm white fish (cod, grouper)
- 2 ripe mangoes
- 6-8 limes
- 1-2 chiles de arbol
- a handful of chopped cilantro

Thinly slice onion & soak in bowl of water with 1 tbsp salt (15 min.) Rinse & drain

Cut the fish & mango into 1" cubes.

Combine the fish, mango & onion in a bowl & squeeze limes over all, evenly covering with lime juice. Stir.

Cover & refrigerate for at least 2 hours. The fish will appear white when "cooked" by lime juice.

Thinly slice chile, add to ceviche with cilantro, salt & pepper.

El Ceviche de San Miguel de Allende

serves 6

2 bay leaves
3 cloves of garlic
2 large white onions
Salt and pepper to taste
4 medium fillets of white fish
10 diced tomatoes
a handful of cilantro leaves
1 tablespoon of dried oregano
½ cup fresh lime juice
1 can of sliced jalapeños
½ cup mayo

MAYONESA

Jalapeños

① Bring 6 cups of water to boil, add bay leaves, 3 garlic cloves, ½ onion, peeled, salt, pepper & 4 fillets of fish.

② When fish flakes apart, remove from water & break into bits in large bowl.

③ Dice remaining 1 & ½ onions & add it along with tomato cilantro, oregano & lime juice to bowl.

④ Pour in jalapeños, & ½ the liquid from the can (vinegar)

⑤ Mix in the mayo, add salt & pepper.

⑥ Serve in small bowls & eat with crackers or totopos (tortilla chips)

Ceviche

de Camarón
Serves 6

SHRIMP CEVICHE ECUADORIAN STYLE

a delicious soup-style ceviche served with
TOSTONES/CHIFLES★ and/or TOSTADO/CHULPE★ or cangil (popcorn)

2 lbs fresh shrimp, shell-on
6 roma tomatoes, diced
3 cups lime juice
1 cup orange juice

1 large red onion, sliced
3 tbsp oil
3 tbsp ketchup, optional
1 cup chopped cilantro
salt & pepper

1 Boil a pot of water & flash cook shrimp, removing shrimp just as they turn pink.

2 Rinse shrimp in cold water to stop cooking process.

3 Peel & devein shrimp, save shells.

4 Put shrimp shells & one tomato in blender Blend until smooth.

5 Using cheese cloth, strain liquid into bowl. Keep liquid, discard shells.

6 Cut shrimp in half (lengthwise).

7 Combine lime & orange juices with liquid from blender in large bowl; add shrimp, remaining tomatoes, onion, oil, ketchup (if desired) & cilantro.

8 Add salt & pepper to taste; serve in small bowls. Often served with a portion of white rice, in addition to crunchy toppings.

Ceviche de Pescado
con Toronja y Palmitas

FISH CEVICHE with Grapefruit & Hearts of Palm

Ceviche is best when it's served the day you prepare it. Medium shrimp or fresh scallops cut into ½" pieces can be substituted for the fish. Always use the freshest seafood as possible.

Ingredients

- 1 lb. firm white fish, cut into bite-sized pieces (grouper or sea bass)
- 1 large red grapefruit, halved (one half juiced, the other half peeled, seeded & cut into bite sized pieces)
- 2 limes (one juiced, the other cut into wedges).
- 1 ½ tbsp olive oil
- 1 tsp soy sauce
- ¼ tsp salt, or to taste
- ¼ tsp ground pepper
- 1 can (15oz) hearts of palm, drained & cut ¼" round slices
- 3 tbsp finely chopped red onion (soaked in a small bowl of ice water for at least 15 minutes then drain).
- ½ jalapeño, seeded & finely diced
- 2 tbsp finely chopped cilantro leaves, plus a handful of whole leaves for garnish.
- Sliced avocado for garnish.

1. Place fish pieces in one layer in a glass dish, add the grapefruit juice & half of the lime juice. Refrigerate for 1 hour or until fish is white throughout.

2. Remove the ceviche from the fridge & drain off the excess juice in the dish. Gently squeeze the fish with your hands, to take out as much juice as possible so it doesn't over marinate.

3. In a large bowl, whisk together the olive oil, soy sauce, the remaining lime juice, salt & pepper.

4. Add the reserved chopped grapefruit, hearts of palm, red onion, jalapeño, fish, & chopped cilantro. Mix together gently.

5. Top each serving with avocado slices & cilantro leaves; serve with lime wedges.

Salsas, Ensaladas
& Adicionales
sauces salads & sides

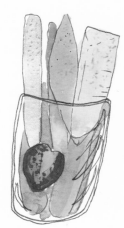

Salsa Roja

makes 3 cups

- 2 pounds ripe tomatoes
- 1-2 jalapeños, cut lengthwise
- 6 cloves garlic, unpeeled
- ½ tsp salt, or to taste
- ½ cup finely chopped white onion
- ¼ cup chopped cilantro

1. Line a skillet with a sheet of aluminum foil & heat over high heat.

2. Roast the tomatoes on the aluminum, turning every 1 min., to blacken the skin. When at least 50% of the tomato skin is roasted & blackened, remove from pan.

3. Remove foil then add jalapeños & garlic & roast over high heat until they are soft & blackened.

4. Peel the garlic and, using a large mortar & pestle, crush it with the jalapeño & salt to make a chunky paste. Add the tomatoes & onion & crush to combine. If the mortar gets too full, transfer to a bowl. Add cilantro & more salt if needed.

SALSA VERDE

- 10 tomatillos • 2 jalapeños
- ½ cup cilantro • 2 cloves garlic
- salt

1. Remove papery husks & wash tomatillos.

2. Cook tomatillos and whole jalapeños in boiling water for 5 minutes, drain.

3. In blender, combine tomatillos jalapeños, cilantro & garlic, Blend to desired texture. Add salt to taste.

Variation: leave the tomatillos & jalapeños raw for a quick, fresh SALSA VERDE

RED CINNAMON SALSA

- ½ white onion
- ½ serrano chile
- 1 clove garlic
- 3 large tomatoes
- 1 tsp cinnamon
- salt & pepper to taste

- Thinly slice onion, set aside. I use a mandoline for this.

- Devein & remove seeds of chile. Mince chile & garlic & cook lightly in oil to soften.

- While chile & garlic are cooking, blend tomatoes & cinnamon in food processor or blender.

- Combine tomatoes, chile & garlic in bowl. Then add sliced onions & season with salt & pepper. Mix & serve.

My friend Rosa Sanabria of San Miguel de Allende, Mexico, taught me this salsa during our 3 weeks of cooking together. The cinnamon gives this salsa a very unique flavor & is delicious served on chiles rellenos.*

GUACAMOLE

serves 6

- 3 ripe avocados
- juice from 2 limes
- ½ cup white onion, finely diced
- 2 cloves garlic, minced
- small handful cilantro, chopped
- salt to taste

Slice avocados & spoon into bowl, add lime juice, mash to desired consistency.
Combine all ingredients with avocado, stir.

Guac. is best if served fresh!

Pico de Gallo de
TUNAS
green prickly pear

- ◆ 4 tunas, green & firm
- ◆ 1 dried guajillo chile toasted on stove
- ◆ 1 onion, diced
- ◆ 1 avocado, diced
- ◆ ¼ cup minced cilantro
- ◆ juice from one lime
- ◆ 1 tsp oregano

- • Peel the tunas, cut in half & scoop out most of the seeds, dice.
- • Crumble the chile into bowl.
- • Add the diced tunas, onion, avocado, cilantro, lime juice & oregano.
- • Season with salt & pepper.

✳ See *Eating Cactus*✳ for more about the *tuna* (prickly pear).

Smoky chile
PASILLA SALSA
○ 3 dried pasilla chiles
○ 1 medium sized tomato
○ ½ large yellow onion
○ ½ cup cilantro
○ 2 cloves garlic
○ salt

1. Heat dried chiles on comál or flat skillet until crispy & fragrant, flipping occasionally. (5 min)

2. Combine all ingredients in blender, blend until smooth. Add salt to taste.

Serves 2-4

Guajillo & caramelized onion Relish

serves 4

- 2 guajillo chiles, whole (remove stem)
- 4 tbsp olive oil
- 1 large yellow onion, diced
- 3 cloves garlic, minced
- 1 lime, juiced
- ½ cup cilantro, chopped
- Salt to taste

Heat chiles in 1 tbsp olive oil in pan, both sides. Remove from pan, set aside.

Sauté onion, garlic & remaining olive oil in the same pan until soft & caramelized.

In food processor, blend chile, onions, garlic, lime juice, until chunky.

Transfer the mixture to a bowl, stir in the cilantro, & season with salt.

{ Serve with meat, seafood in a quesadilla or in a taco }

Chimichurri

a vinegar-based sauce to serve with meat, fish and rice, commonly eaten in Argentina.

2 cups cilantro
2 cups parsley
3 cloves raw garlic
½ cup white vinegar

½ cup olive oil
1 pinch chile pepper flakes
1 pinch oregano
salt & pepper

Finely chop cilantro, parsley & garlic; combine with vinegar & olive oil.

Add chile pepper, oregano, salt & pepper to taste.

Can use food processor to blend.

Creamy Cilantro Dip

a typical side with Cuban Mariquitas* (plantain chips) & yuca fries.

½ cup sour cream or mayonnaise
1 cup cilantro leaves
juice of one lime
½ jalapeño

2 tbsp white vinegar
salt & pepper to taste

Combine all in blender or food processor.
Use immediately or refrigerate until ready to serve.

Aji Criollo

- 4 ajís: small hot chiles, thai bird chiles or chile de arbol, chopped
- 1 jalapeño, deveined & seeded
- 2 cloves garlic
- ¼ cup water
- ¼ cup olive oil
- 2 green onions, chopped
- 2 handfuls cilantro
- Pinch of salt

- Blend together chiles, garlic & water in a blender or food processor.
- Transfer to bowl & add olive oil, green onion, cilantro & salt.

Ají de tomate de arbol

- 5-7 tomate de arbol,* fresh or frozen
- 2-3 ají, thai chile, chile de arbol or habañero, seeded.
- ¼ cup water
- ¼ cup white onion
- juice from ½ lime
- 1 handful cilantro, chopped
- Pinch of salt

two typical hot sauces found on the tables of

Ecuador

- If using fresh, peel tomate de arbol & blend with chiles & ¼ cup water. If frozen, defrost first then scoop out insides & blend (discard peel).
- Transfer chile & tomate de arbol to saucepan & cook over medium heat for 10 minutes.
- Remove from heat & add onion, lime juice, cilantro & salt to taste.

★ Tomate de arbol is native to the Andean region. The fruit is acidic & firm, & has seeds larger than a tomato. Can usually be found in the frozen section in Latin american groceries.

Mojo* SAUCE

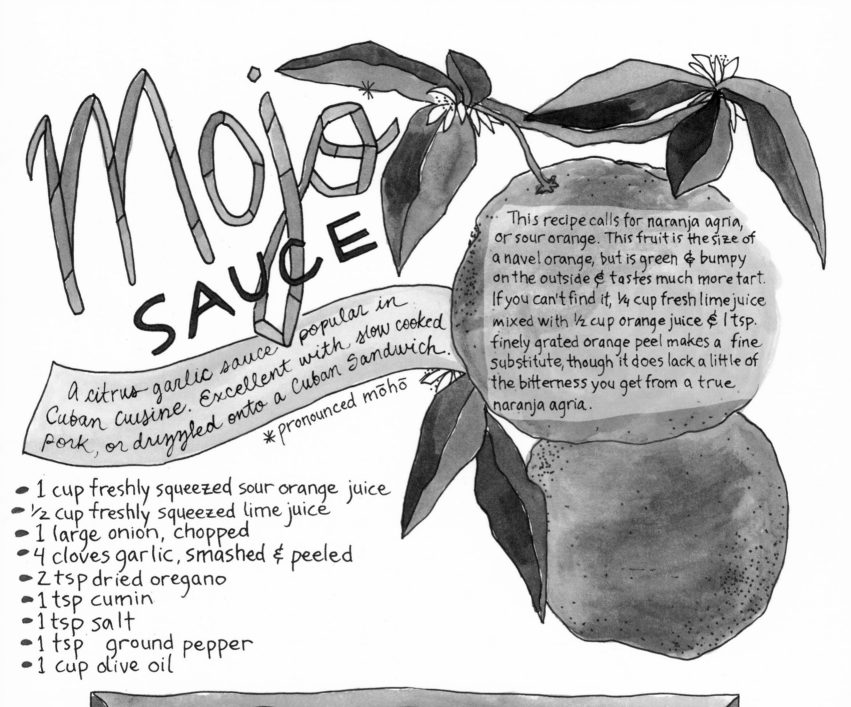

A citrus garlic sauce popular in Cuban cuisine. Excellent with slow cooked pork, or drizzled onto a Cuban Sandwich.

*pronounced mōhō

This recipe calls for naranja agria, or sour orange. This fruit is the size of a navel orange, but is green & bumpy on the outside & tastes much more tart. If you can't find it, ¼ cup fresh lime juice mixed with ½ cup orange juice & 1 tsp. finely grated orange peel makes a fine substitute, though it does lack a little of the bitterness you get from a true naranja agria.

- 1 cup freshly squeezed sour orange juice
- ½ cup freshly squeezed lime juice
- 1 large onion, chopped
- 4 cloves garlic, smashed & peeled
- 2 tsp dried oregano
- 1 tsp cumin
- 1 tsp salt
- 1 tsp ground pepper
- 1 cup olive oil

① Using a food processor or blender, puree the sour orange juice, lime juice, onion, garlic, oregano, cumin, salt & pepper until it forms a smooth paste. (1 min)

② While blending, slowly add olive oil until the mojo sauce is fully emulsified.

③ Store & use from sealed container for up to three weeks.

Chipotle Chile ADOBO SAUCE

Store this sauce Use as a marinade for meats & as a base for stews & rice dishes. MAKES 8 CUPS

- ½ lb dried chipotle chiles
  try MECOS which look like tan suede or MORITAS which are smaller & dark red. Both are spicy & smoky.
- 1 lb roma tomatoes
- 1 cup olive oil
- 3 carrots, sliced
- 1 large white onion, sliced thinly
- 6 garlic cloves, sliced
- 2 sprigs fresh thyme
- 2 bay leaves

- 2 whole cloves
- ½ tsp cinnamon
- ½ tsp cumin
- ½ cup piloncillo, grated
- 1 tsp salt
- 1 ½ cups white vinegar

1. Place chipotles & whole tomatoes in a sauce pan & cover with water. Bring to a boil & cook over medium heat until tomatoes are soft but not falling apart, about 15 minutes. Remove from heat & drain, reserving 1 cup cooking liquid.

2. Blend the cooked tomatoes & half of the chiles with 1 cup of the cooking liquid until smooth. (Set aside the other whole chiles)

3. Heat 1 cup olive oil in a large pan. Add carrots & sliced onions & cook for 5 minutes, then add garlic.

4. Pour tomato/chile purée into the pan & add thyme, bay leaves, cloves, cinnamon, cumin, piloncillo & salt. Simmer for 8-10 minutes.

5. Stir in vinegar & reserved chipotles, then simmer for 10 more min.

6. Remove thyme sprigs & bay leaves, & let Adobo cool. Store in canning jars, refrigerated.

ACEITE de ACHIOTE

ANNATO OIL

Heat 1-1½ tbsp achiote seeds with ½ cup olive oil over medium heat. Oil will become a yellow/orange color within about 5 minutes. Remove from heat & strain. Drain seeds, save oil in bottle to use in food as a natural colorant for dishes, including rice & potatoes.

Achiote is also sold "molido" or ground. It can be added directly to your recipe, turning the food a golden color upon stirring in the powder.

Chile Oil

a medium-hot chile sauce for the table

- 10-15 chiles de arbol, dried • ⅓ cup olive oil • pinch of salt

Remove stem & seeds from chiles
Combine with olive oil & blend.
Heat the mixture on stove for
5-10 minutes, stir & add salt.

Chile oil is something I make & save in a jar, enjoying it over 1-2 weeks served on tacos, beans & rice or anything that needs an extra kick. Heating the chiles really brings out the flavor.

ENSALADA de NOPALES

- 4 nopales pads
- 1 tomato, diced
- 1 lime, juiced
- ½ serrano chile, minced
- 1 white onion, sliced
- 3 tbsp olive oil
- handful cilantro leaves
- queso cotija (optional)

1. Rinse off the nopal & using a kitchen scrubbie or reverse side of sponge scrub away from the base of the spines. Cut off remaining spines with paring knife.

2. Trim edges of nopal, then dice.

3. Boil water & add diced nopales. Cook for 10 min, color will change to a dull green. Rinse well, then strain. Or skip this step & enjoy raw (crunchier).

4. Cool nopales, then add tomato, lime, chile, onion, olive oil, salt & cilantro. Mix & serve.

A nopal is part of the Opuntia family cultivated centuries ago in Central Mexico.

Nopales salad is great in a taco or served alongside meat, seafood or grilled chicken. I enjoy scrambling nopales with an egg & serving with toast or in a torta.
(a mexican sandwich)

84

Black Bean, Citrus Sweet Pepper SALAD

4-6 SERVINGS

- 2-3 Red/yellow/orange peppers, diced
- 2 cups cooked black beans (or 16 oz can)
- ½ cup red onion, finely chopped
- 1-2 cloves garlic, minced
- 1 handful fresh basil, chopped
- 1 handful fresh flat leaf parsley, chopped
- 2 tbsp. olive oil
- 2 tbsp. red wine vinegar
- 1 tsp. orange zest
- Salt & pepper to taste

Toss everything together in a large bowl, add salt & pepper to taste.

Let stand for 20 min. in refrigerator before serving.

Chayote & Jicama Salad with Cilantro Lime Vinaigrette

serves 4
INGREDIENTS

- Juice of 1 lime
- ¼ cup olive oil
- ¼ cup red wine vinegar
- ¼ cup chopped clantro
- 1 tbsp salt, or to taste
- ¼ tsp sugar

- 1 red onion, thinly sliced
- 1 chayote (1lb), pitted & julienned
- 1 jicama (1lb) peeled & julienned
- 4 radishes, thinly sliced

1 Whisk together lime juice, olive oil, vinegar, cilantro, salt & sugar.

2 Pour mixture over onions & let marinate for 10-15 minutes.

3 Combine julienned chayote, jicama & radishes in a large bowl & toss together with dressed onions.

serve immediately, enjoy!

AVOCADOS
in the HALF SHELL
WITH Red Quinoa Salad

SERVES 6

1 CUP RED QUINOA

2 CUPS WATER

1 CUP ROASTED TOMATO SALSA*

½ tsp SALT

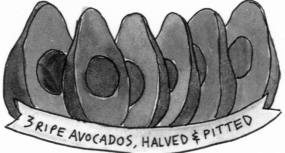

3 RIPE AVOCADOS, HALVED & PITTED

¼ CUP CHOPPED GREEN ONION

1. Bring quinoa & water to a boil then reduce heat to a simmer. Cover & cook until all the water is absorbed (15 minutes) then let cool.

2. In a large bowl, combine the quinoa, 1 cup roasted tomato salsa,* green onions & salt, stir.

3. Using a tablespoon, generously fill the cavity of each avocado half; the dish can be enjoyed right out of the shell. The quinoa salad looks like a pit, but one that can be eaten!

4. Serve avocados on a platter, adding extra salad to the center of the dish.

Avocado Mango Lettuce Wraps

1 tsp minced SERRANO CHILE

2 MANGOES

2 HEADS BUTTER LETTUCE

2 RED ONIONS

2 LIMES

3 AVOCADOS

SALT to taste

① Cut onions in half, thinly slice, soak in bowl of water with 1 tbsp salt for 15 min. Rinse & drain.

② Cut mangoes in half lengthwise, discard seed. Slice into ½" cubes inside peel, then flip peel inside out and remove fruit.

③ Dice avocados and combine with mangoes and onions in bowl with juice of 2 limes, toss together.

④ Add minced serrano chile and salt to taste

⑤ Place 2-4 tbsp salad on lettuce leaf. Serve immediately

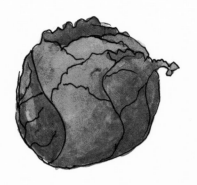

Curtido

CABBAGE
COLESLAW

¼ cup white vinegar
¼ cup olive oil
¼ cup fresh squeezed orange juice
¼ cup fresh lime juice
½ head red/green/savoy cabbage
½ Red onion, cut in half & sliced
Handful chopped cilantro
Salt & pepper to taste

- Mix together vinegar, olive oil, orange & lime juices. Combine with cabbage (shredded) & onion in bowl.
- Toss in cilantro, add salt & pepper to taste.

Let stand for 20 min. before serving to allow flavors to meld & cabbage to soften.

Serves 6 prep time 30 mins

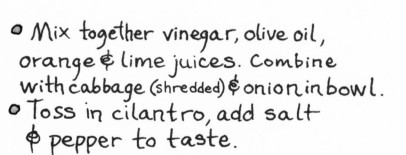

Remolacha
Beet salad

- 3 beets
- 1 carrot, julienned
- 2 tbsp mayonnaise
- 1 tbsp lime juice
- 2 tbsp chopped cilantro

Lightly steam beets, then dice. Add cut carrot, mayo, lime juice & cilantro to beets in bowl, mix. Add salt to taste.

serves 4, prep time: 20 min.

TOMATO lime ONION

an essential garnish & side dish for many Andean favorites.

known as
Encebollado

- 1 large red onion
- 3 tomatoes
- salt
- 1 lime

- Slice onion & soak in bowl of water with 2 tbsp salt for 15 mins.

  This step helps to mellow the sharp raw onion flavor.

- Strain & rinse well.

- Dice tomatoes, combine with onion, lime juice & salt to taste.

- Let rest for 10 mins before serving

typically served with fish, llapingachos*
boiled yuca* & encebollado soup*

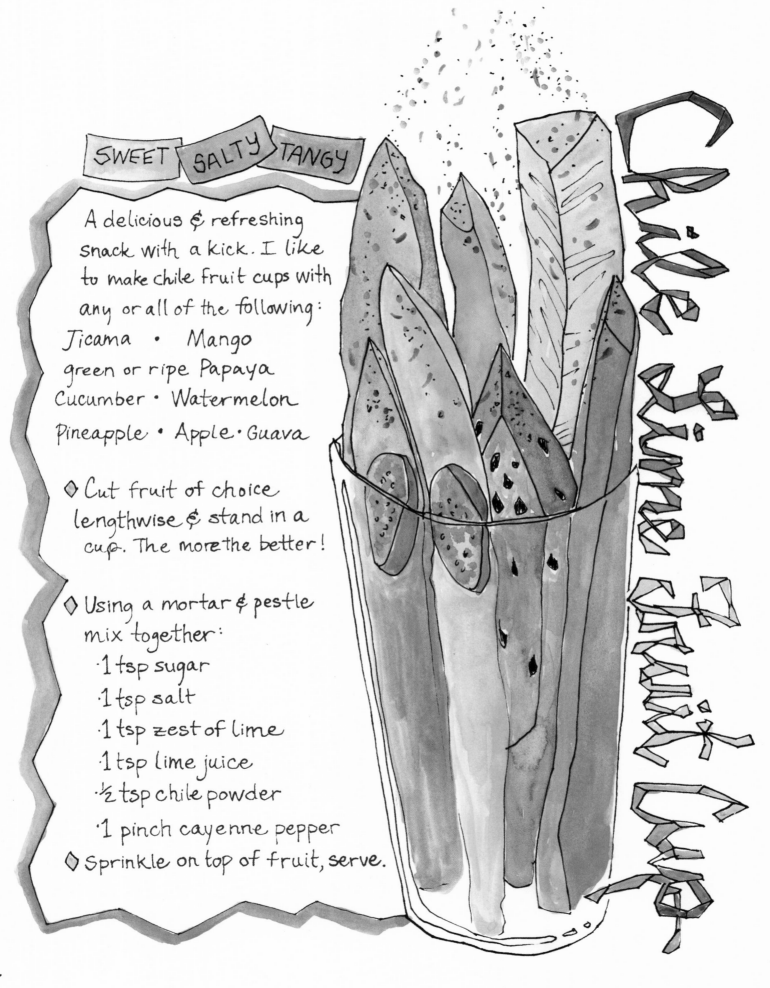

SWEET SALTY TANGY

Chile Lime Fruit Cup

A delicious & refreshing snack with a kick. I like to make chile fruit cups with any or all of the following:
Jicama • Mango
green or ripe Papaya
Cucumber • Watermelon
Pineapple • Apple • Guava

◊ Cut fruit of choice lengthwise & stand in a cup. The more the better!

◊ Using a mortar & pestle mix together:
· 1 tsp sugar
· 1 tsp salt
· 1 tsp zest of lime
· 1 tsp lime juice
· ½ tsp chile powder
· 1 pinch cayenne pepper

◊ Sprinkle on top of fruit, serve.

Chile Lime Corn on the Cob with Queso Fresco

serves 6

for the grill

- 1 jalapeño
- ¾ cup crema Mexicana (similar to crème fraîche)
- 6 ears of corn, husk on
- chile powder
- 1 cup cotija cheese (crumbly queso fresco)
- 1-2 limes, cut in wedges
- salt

- Roast jalapeño, peel skin, devein & remove seeds, then mince.
- Mix jalapeño with crema, let stand for 1 hour.
- Peel back the outer corn leaves & tie back with string to create a handle. Keep inner leaves on while grilling.
- Roast the corn until steamed & lightly charred.
- Remove or peel back the inner leaves & spread a thin layer of crema on corn. Sprinkle a bit of chile powder & quickly roll in cojita cheese. Squeeze lime wedge & add a touch of salt. Enjoy immediately!

PLATANITOS MARIQUITAS
CHIFLES
PLANTAIN CHIPS

Best Served Hot!

- 2 green plantains
- 1 cup vegetable oil

Cut lengthwise just through peel, remove green peel.

Thinly cut starchy plantain in thin vertical strips or disks, cut with a mandoline if available. Fry in oil, flipping until golden brown. Blot with paper towel salt to taste—

serves 6, prep time 30min

patacones
·TOSTONES· THICK PLANTAIN CHIPS

4 green plantains, veggie oil, salt

- Peel plantain & cut it into 1½" pieces. The easiest way to do this is to cut both ends off, then slice the peel down one side, barely cutting into fruit, then peel.
- Heat 1" veggie oil, fry on both sides until golden brown. Remove & blot with paper towel.
- Smash each with the bottom of a coffee mug to flatten. Fry both sides again until golden brown.
- Remove from oil, blot well with paper towel.
- Lightly salt, serve immediately.

Panamanians eat patacones with ketchup & they are an essential side to black beans in Cuba. I learned to make these in Quito, Ecuador, where we prepared them to complement Manestra (lentils) & rice.

¡YUCA!

A starchy root vegetable native to South America.
Yuca can be made into a satisfying side dish: boiled, fried,
or prepared as chips. It is more nutritious than a potato —
rich in calcium, vitamin C & phosphorous.
Always cook yuca before eating.

- 2 large yuca
- 2 tbsp salt
- Veggie/peanut oil

▷ Peel the waxed brown skin, then quarter the root
   lengthwise.   Cut in 4" sections.

▷ Boil the yuca in water with 2 tbsp salt for a ½ hour or
   until it can easily be pierced with a fork.
   I serve boiled yuca with ají or chimichurri★
sauce & it goes well with grilled meat.

▷ To fry, heat 1" of veggie/peanut oil in pan, add chunks
   of boiled yuca.   Fry until golden on all sides.
▷ Transfer to paper towel, sprinkle with salt.

Yuca Chips

- ◎ Peel skin & thinly slice yuca root,
   using mandoline if available.
- ◎ Fry yuca chips in ½" frying oil,
   flipping to evenly cook until golden.
- ◎ Transfer to paper towel, sprinkle with salt & serve.

Muchines de Yuca
stuffed cassava fritters

CRUNCHY FRIED OUTSIDE

SOFT YUMMY FILLING

MAKES 12 MUCHINES

2 large yuca roots, 1 egg, 1 tsp salt
1 cup cheese, 1 cup veggie oil:
Try queso blanco or fresh goat cheese.

Peel & finely grate yuca. Squeeze out water from yuca over sink in handfuls. Beat an egg & mix it well with yuca & salt. Place 1 tbsp yuca in palm & press cheese in middle. Cover with more yuca, enclosing cheese in plump disk shape, 2" wide. Fry until golden brown, flipping to cook both sides. Blot with paper towel & serve immediately.

I learned how to make these from Anita Gomez in Quito, Ecuador. Anita likes to serve these with honey, which makes them a delicious sweet treat.

97

TOSTADO · CHULPE

CORN THAT POPS BUT DOESN'T BURST LIKE POPCORN

serves 4 prep time 20 min

- 3 tbsp veggie oil
- 2 cups chulpe, presoaked in water (10 min)
- 1 yellow onion, diced

Heat oil in pan, add chulpe kernels. Shake pan at times to evenly heat. Once chulpe starts to pop, add onion to pan then cover with lid & continue to shake pan. Onions should be crispy. Salt to taste. Great snack!

This crunchy snack made of corn called "cancha" can usually be found in Latin American groceries that carry South American food. Chulpe is the S. American "Corn Nut".

Chile Cheese CORN BREAD

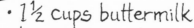

- 1 cup cornmeal
- 1 cup white flour
- 2 tsp baking powder
- ½ tsp baking soda
- 1 tsp salt
- 2 eggs

- 1½ cups buttermilk
- ⅓ cup olive oil
- 1½ cups grated monterey jack cheese
- 1 cup fresh corn (frozen okay)
- 3 jalapeño chiles, diced

1. Preheat oven to 375°
2. Mix together cornmeal, flour, baking powder, baking soda & salt.
3. Beat together eggs, buttermilk & olive oil.
4. Combine wet & dry ingredients & add grated cheese, corn & chiles (seeded & deveined) to bowl. Mix.
5. Grease skillet or pan, pour in batter & cook in oven for 20-30 minutes. After 20 minutes insert toothpick in center of cornbread. If it comes out clean, remove from oven.
6. Let stand for 20 minutes before serving.

a family favorite that's full of flavor!
ENJOY WITH A HEARTY SOUP LIKE *Locro de Zapallo*

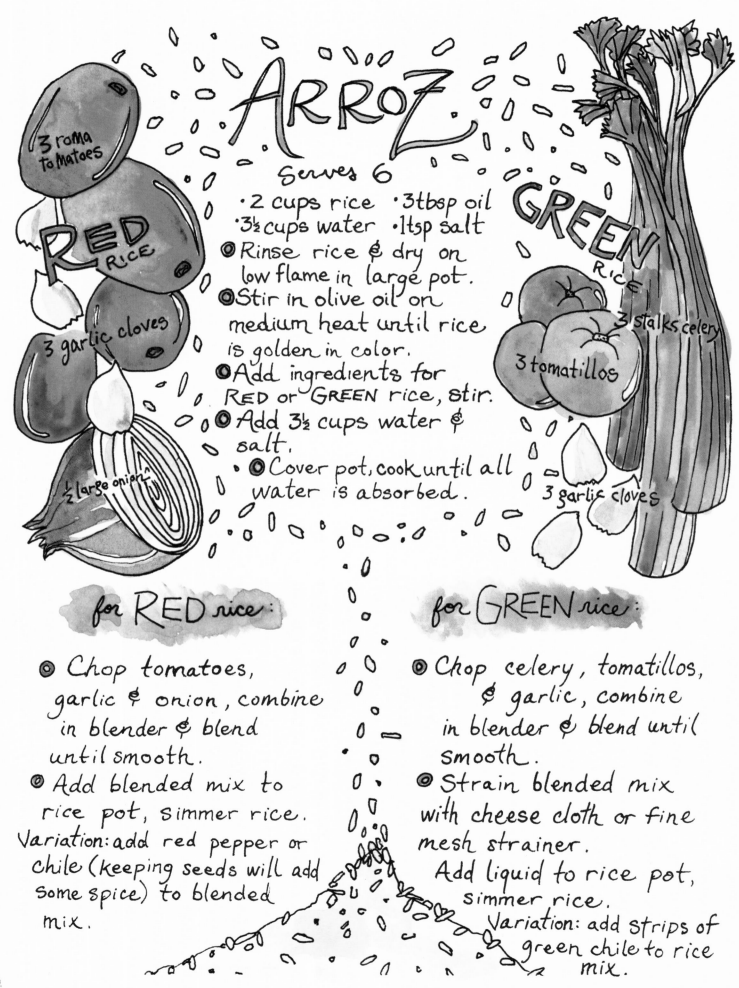

ARROZ

Serves 6

- 2 cups rice
- 3½ cups water
- 3 tbsp oil
- 1 tsp salt

RED RICE

- 3 roma tomatoes
- 3 garlic cloves
- ½ large onion

GREEN RICE

- 3 tomatillos
- 3 stalks celery
- 3 garlic cloves

◎ Rinse rice & dry on low flame in large pot.

◎ Stir in olive oil on medium heat until rice is golden in color.

◎ Add ingredients for RED or GREEN rice, stir.

◎ Add 3½ cups water & salt.

◎ Cover pot, cook until all water is absorbed.

for RED rice:

◎ Chop tomatoes, garlic & onion, combine in blender & blend until smooth.

◎ Add blended mix to rice pot, simmer rice.

Variation: add red pepper or chile (keeping seeds will add some spice) to blended mix.

for GREEN rice:

◎ Chop celery, tomatillos, & garlic, combine in blender & blend until smooth.

◎ Strain blended mix with cheese cloth or fine mesh strainer.

Add liquid to rice pot, simmer rice.

Variation: add strips of green chile to rice mix.

MANESTRA DE LENTEJA
con Arroz Amarillo
STEWED LENTILS WITH YELLOW RICE

MANESTRA INGREDIENTS

- 2 tbsp olive oil
- 2 tomatoes
- 1 large red onion, diced
- 1 large bell pepper, diced
- 6 garlic cloves, diced
- 1 tbsp achiote oil *
- 2 tsp ground cumin
- 1 tsp salt
- 6½ cups water
- 2 cups lentils, rinsed
- 1 green plantain, peeled & grated
- ½ cup chopped cilantro

1. Heat the oil in a pot over medium heat. Add the tomatoes, onion, pepper, garlic, achiote oil, cumin & salt & cook (6-8 min.)

2. Add the water & bring to a boil. Add the lentils, reduce the heat to medium low & cook, covered, for 10 minutes.

3. Stir in the grated plantain. This will thicken the lentils & add a distinctive flavor. Continue to cook until the lentils are soft (30-45 min). Stir in the cilantro, & season with salt, if needed.

ARROZ AMARILLO INGREDIENTS

- 2 tbsp extra virgin olive oil or butter
- 2 tbsp minced white onions
- 2 garlic cloves, minced
- 1 tsp ground achiote (annatto)
- ½ tsp salt
- 2 cups long grain white rice
- 3 cups water

1. Heat the oil in the saucepan over medium heat. Add the onions, garlic, achiote & salt & cook until soft (2-4 min).

2. Add the rice & stir to coat with the oil & achiote. Add the water & bring rice to a boil. Cook until the water covers the rice by about ¼", then cover, reduce the heat to low & cook until tender (20 min.)

3. To serve, fill a small bowl with rice & pack it down gently. Place a plate on top

Remove bowl, then add manestra (stewed lentils) & sides of choice around the rice.

- ⊚ ají criollo *
- ⊚ arroz amarillo
- ⊚ manestra
- ⊚ fried plantains *
- ⊚ grilled chicken, pork or steak
- ⊚ avocado
- ⊚ tomato & onion encebollado salad *

Frijoles

Refritos · REFRIED BEANS · serves 6

- 2½ cups dried beans*
- Water
- 3 avocado leaves, dried
- 1 tsp cumin seeds
- 1 white onion, thinly sliced
- 3 cloves garlic, smashed

- olive oil
- 1 jalapeño, roasted & diced
- salt to taste
- cotija cheese

  *Try an heirloom variety, ayocote beans are delicious.

1. Put the beans in a large bowl & add water to cover by 2". Soak overnight.

2. Drain the beans & put in pot with avocado leaves & 8 cups water. Bring to a boil, then simmer until soft (1-2 hours).

3. While beans are cooking, toast the cumin seeds in a pan, then grind the seeds with a mortar & pestle.

4. Sauté the onions & smashed garlic in 1 tsp olive oil in a pan until soft.

5. Drain the beans & discard the avocado leaves. If you have one, mix & mash with a metate (otherwise use a potato masher), adding sautéed onions, cumin seeds & roasted jalapeños as you mash the beans.

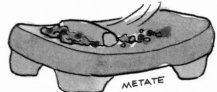
METATE

6. Heat 3 tbsp olive oil in a clean pan & add beans to warm them before serving. Season with salt.

Serve with cotija cheese & fresh tortillas.

my favorite BLACK BEANS

serves 6

One of 500 varieties of kidney beans, black beans have been a food staple for over 7,000 years in Central & South America.

- Cover dry beans with water & soak overnight.
- Bring 8 c. water to boil; add drained beans & reduce heat. Cook until soft (1-1½ hours). I use a large cast iron pot, but a pressure cooker (20-25 mins. to cook) or crock pot works well too.
- Mash garlic with mortar & pestle, sauté with onions & peppers in olive oil until soft, then add to beans.
- Add cumin, oregano & bay leaves. Simmer for at least a ½ hour.
- Take out about 1 cup of beans & mash them up, then add back in.
- Remove bay leaves, salt & pepper to taste. Add vinegar ✳
- Mince garnishes of choice, serve black beans over rice about ½ hour after removing from heat.

- 2½ c. black beans
- 8 c. water
- 3 cloves garlic
- 1½ c. chopped white onion
- 1 large bell pepper, chopped
- 4 tbsp olive oil
- 1 tsp cumin
- 1 tsp oregano
- 2 bay leaves
- 3 tbsp white vinegar

epazote
cilantro } optional garnishes
green onion }

- While in Costa Rica I ate black beans often with patacones*, an excellant crunchy side dish that scoops the beans up well.

✳ Acid makes the outside of the beans tough. Therefore it's best to add vinegar or citrus at the end.

103

Bebidas

drinks

Agua Fresca

- 3 cups fresh fruit (about 1 cantaloupe)
- 3 cups water (agua)
- sugar or honey to taste

Combine fruit & water in blender, purée. Pour purée through strainer, separating pulp from agua. Add sweetener of choice, serve chilled.

VARIATIONS INCLUDE Strawberry, watermelon, pineapple, guava, passionfruit

cool & delicious Refrescos

ICED GINGER TEA

- 1×2" piece of fresh ginger
- 4 cups water
- juice from ½ lemon
- honey to taste

Peel the ginger root into thin slices.
Boil 4 cups water & add ginger.
Cover & simmer for about 20 minutes.
Pour through a strainer.
Add *lemon* juice & honey to taste, serve chilled.

Jengibre

HIBISCUS ICED TEA

- 6 cups water
- 1 cup dried hibiscus flowers
- juice from ½ orange
- 2-4 tbsp sugar/honey/agave syrup
- 1 lime sliced in wedges

Boil 4 cups water, add hibiscus flowers.
Remove from heat, let stand for 20 min.
Strain into pitcher, discard hibiscus blossoms.
Add 2 cups water, orange juice & desired
sweetener. Serve over ice with lime wedges.

Flor de Jamaica

TAMARIND AGUA FRESCA

- 6 cups water
- 8 oz (2 big handfuls) tamarind pods, peeled
- 2-4 tbsp sugar to taste

Boil 4 cups water, add peeled tamarind.
Simmer for 5-10 minutes. Cool.
Break apart the tamarind seed & pulp with
potato masher. Pass through strainer
into pitcher, discard pulp. Add 2 cups water
& sugar to taste. Serve chilled.

Tamarindo

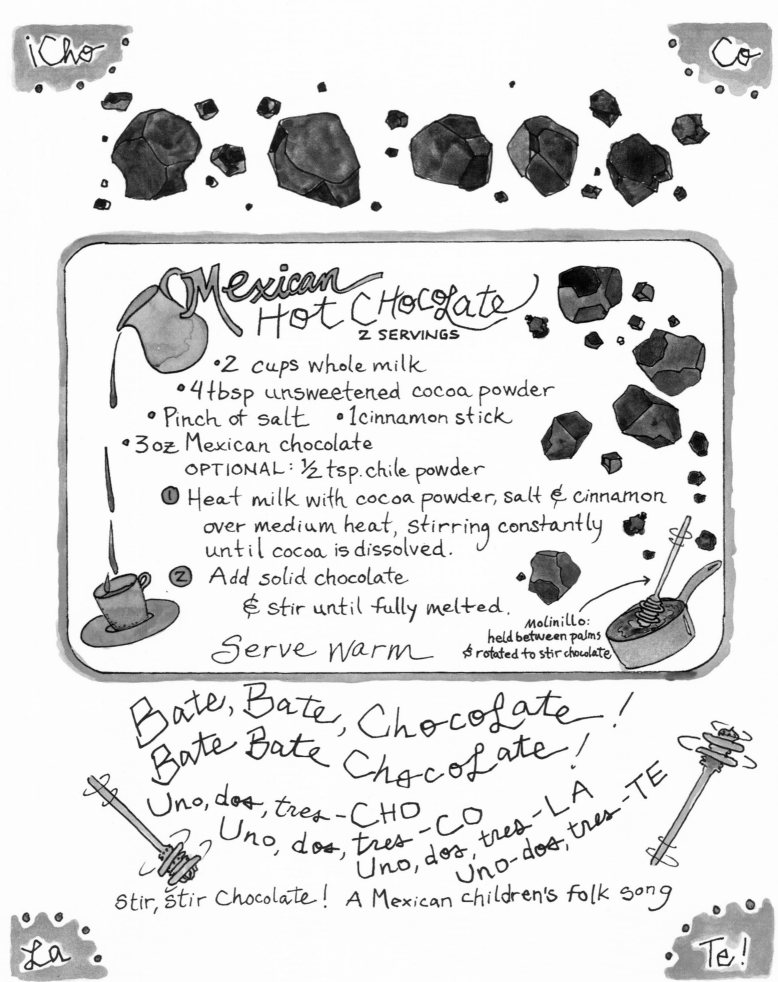

Mexican Hot Chocolate
2 SERVINGS

- 2 cups whole milk
- 4 tbsp unsweetened cocoa powder
- Pinch of salt   • 1 cinnamon stick
- 3 oz Mexican chocolate

OPTIONAL: ½ tsp. chile powder

1. Heat milk with cocoa powder, salt & cinnamon over medium heat, stirring constantly until cocoa is dissolved.

2. Add solid chocolate & stir until fully melted.

Serve warm

Molinillo: held between palms & rotated to stir chocolate

Bate, Bate, Chocolate!
Bate Bate Chocolate!
Uno, dos, tres - CHO
Uno, dos, tres - CO
Uno, dos, tres - LA
Uno, dos, tres - TE
Uno-dos, tres -TE
Stir, stir Chocolate!   A Mexican children's folk song

HORCHATA

8 servings
prep time: 20 min.

SWEET MEXICAN RICE BEVERAGE

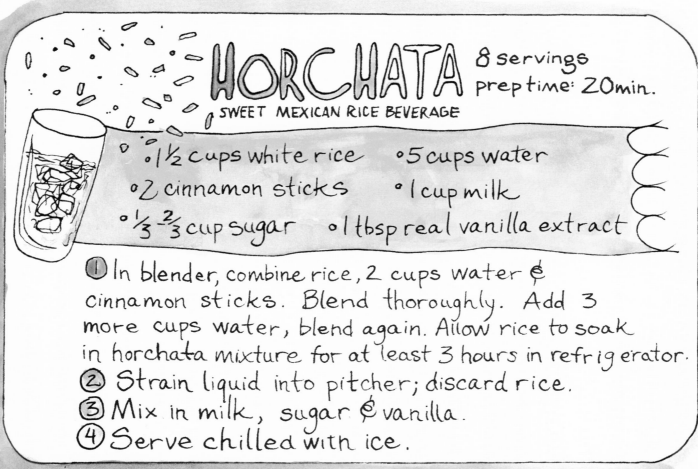

- 1½ cups white rice
- 2 cinnamon sticks
- ⅓ - ⅔ cup sugar
- 5 cups water
- 1 cup milk
- 1 tbsp real vanilla extract

① In blender, combine rice, 2 cups water & cinnamon sticks. Blend thoroughly. Add 3 more cups water, blend again. Allow rice to soak in horchata mixture for at least 3 hours in refrigerator.
② Strain liquid into pitcher; discard rice.
③ Mix in milk, sugar & vanilla.
④ Serve chilled with ice.

This beverage is popular throughout Central America. It is usually tan & opaque but can be made of nuts & seeds, in addition to the version I know made of rice. Some horchatas include milk, others do not. I first enjoyed this beverage at an outdoor market in Oaxaca, Mexico.

Morocho con leche

a sweet warm corn beverage of Ecuador

¼ lb dried cracked corn/morocho
5 cups milk
Rind from ½ an orange
1 cinnamon stick
6 cloves
1 cup sugar or to taste
Rind from ½ a lemon (grated)
2 tsp vanilla extract

SERVES 4

1. Soak the morocho overnight in two times as much water as corn.

2. In a large pan, add milk, drained corn, orange rind, cinnamon & cloves. Simmer for 1.5-2 hours.

3. Add sugar, lemon rind & vanilla, serve hot.

I love morocho on a cold evening or served for breakfast like a hot cereal.

Atole

Sold for one or two pesos a cup, this warm drink is a classic served up by many street vendors in Mexico & Central America. Two common types are the Masa Harina version & the richer, more dessert-like Atole de Maicena (cornstarch). This type can be made by replacing the masa harina with cornstarch & the water with milk.

INGREDIENTS:
- ½ cup masa harina (masa flour) or cornstarch
- 6 cups water or milk
- 1 vanilla bean, split lengthwise
- 1 cinnamon stick
- ¼ cup piloncillo (cane sugar), or ¼ cup brown sugar

① Process masa harina with 2 cups water in blender until smooth.

② Transfer mixture to saucepan & stir in the remaining 4 cups water. Heat on medium.

③ Scrape vanilla bean seeds into the saucepan & add the cinnamon stick, then stir. Mixture will begin to thicken.

④ Add piloncillo (or brown sugar), continue mixing to dissolve sugar.

OPTIONAL: Add 2 tbsp baking chocolate to each serving to make "Champurrado". Or ½ cup chopped strawberries to create an "Atole con Fruta". Both alternatives add additional flavor & texture to the drink.

111

Margarita
de David

SERVES 2

- 3 shots tequila reposado
- 1 shot Cointreau (triple sec)
- 1 shot fresh lime juice   1 jalapeño
- 1 oz fresh squeezed orange juice

① Shake all ingredients except jalapeño with ice cubes in cocktail shaker.

② Serve "up" in a martini glass. For the best margarita, freeze glasses first, then serve.

③ Slice jalapeño, add a couple pieces to each drink.

Variation: Store margarita in freezer for 4-5 hours to enjoy the beverage in a just-before-frozen state.

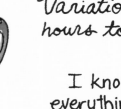

I know many people who are always adding spice to most everything they consume. This recipe is for those characters.

My friend David visited me on one of my trips to Mexico & he whipped up this margarita recipe in my aunt's kitchen one hot afternoon. We slurped down slushy, spicy margaritas as we painted on canvas into the night.

Michelada

serves one

- 1 lime
- salt (for the rim)
- 1 Mexican beer
- 1 dash pepper
- 1 dash soy sauce
- 1 dash worcestershire sauce
- 1-3 dashes hot sauce

1. Salt the rim of the glass by passing a lime wedge over the edge. Dip the glass in a plate covered with salt.

2. Combine all ingredients over ice in a large glass, mix well.

Variation

The lazy person's Michelada

- 1 dark Mexican beer
- ½ cup V8 juice

} serve over ice

Red Wine Sangria

serves 6

2 RIPE PEARS

2 CUPS GINGER ALE

1 BOTTLE FRUITY RED WINE

2 JUICY ORANGES

½ CUP ORANGE JUICE

½ CUP BRANDY

3 LIMES

2 CRISPY APPLES

2 tbsp SUGAR

1 Dice up pears & apples, Slice oranges & limes

save some lime wedges for the edges of serving glasses

2 Combine wine, orange juice, brandy & sugar with fruit. Let stand for 2+ hours.

eat the fruit, it's delicious!

3 Add ginger ale & ice to sangria just before serving.

Mojito

The key to a great mojito is muddling the mint well with the sugar.

1 serving, multiply as needed
- ½ handful fresh mint (I prefer spearmint)
- 2-3 tsp powdered sugar (or sugar cane juice if available)
- 1 shot (2 oz) light or gold rum
- juice from ½ lime, + 1 wedge for garnish
- ice
- Soda water to fill glass

1. Muddle mint & sugar using muddler or mortar & pestle.
2. Add rum & lime juice then ice & soda water, stir.
3. Serve with a lime wedge & if available a stick of sugar cane

Piña Colada

serves 4-6

- 3 cups pineapple juice
- 1 cup white rum
- ½ cup cream of coconut

Stir all the ingredients together in a large pitcher, then add ice. Alternately, you can use a blender to mix then serve over ice & the drink will take on a frappé-like consistency.

Pisco Sour

one serving

2 oz pisco

1 oz fresh lime juice + a lime wedge to serve with drink

½ oz Simple Syrup or to taste. (equal parts water & sugar)

1 egg white

1. Add pisco, lime juice, simple syrup & egg white to a cocktail shaker & fill with ice.
2. Shake well & strain into a glass; sprinkle a few drops of Angostura bitters on top of the foam & make a simple design by swirling the bitters with a straw.

3. Serve with a wedge of lime.

→ Famous in ← Peru & Chile

a dash of Angostura Bitters

Postres
desserts

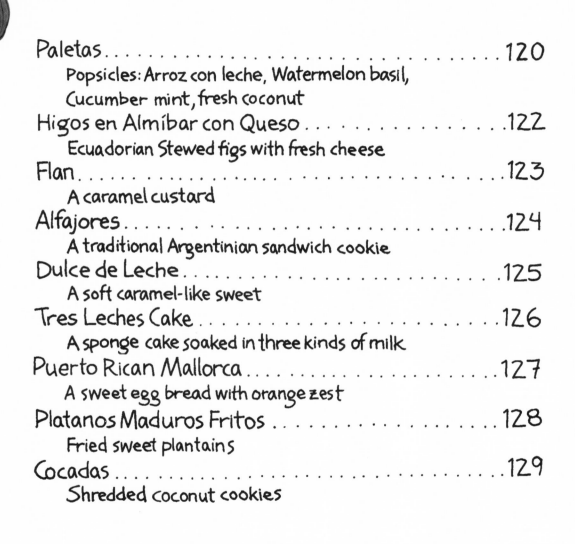

PALETAS
Popsicles

ARROZ CON LECHE PALETAS

- 3 cups whole milk
- 2 cups water
- ¾ cup rice
- 2 cinnamon sticks
- 1 14oz can sweetened condensed milk with 1½ cups water
- 2 tsp vanilla extract
- ¼ tsp salt
- ¼ tsp ground cinnamon

▷ Bring milk & water to a boil & then reduce heat to low (5 min). Stir in rice & cinnamon sticks & simmer, partially covered, until rice is almost tender, 20-30 min.

▷ Remove cinnamon sticks, then stir in the sweetened condensed milk mixture, vanilla extract & salt. Simmer for 10-15 mins. more. Remove from heat, mix in cinnamon & cool.

▷ Pour mixture into 3oz molds. Freeze until halfway frozen (1-2 hours). Insert Popsicle stick into each mold & freeze until solid, about 3 hours more.

WATERMELON BASIL PALETAS

- About 3 cups chopped watermelon
- 1 handful fresh basil
- ½ cup sugar or to taste

▷ Combine all ingredients in blender, strain.
▷ Add liquid to popsicle mold, freeze.

CUCUMBER MINT PALETAS

- 2 medium-sized cucumbers
- 1 handful fresh mint
- ½ cup sugar or to taste
- ¼ cup fresh squeezed lime juice

▹ Combine all ingredients in blender, blend until smooth.

▹ optional: pass mixture through a fine strainer, discard residue.

▹ Add liquid to popsicle mold, freeze.

Alternative popsicle mold: a paper cup
① Freeze w/ liquid
② Peel back the sides as you eat.

FRESH COCONUT PALETAS

- 1 fresh coconut
- 1½ cups hot water
- 2 cups whole milk
- ½ cup sugar
- ¾ tsp salt

▹ Drain the water from the coconut (save for another use) & separate the coconut meat from its shell. (see p. 24) Using a vegetable peeler, shave thin slices of coconut meat until you have about 1 cup. Set aside.

▹ Working in batches blend the remaining coconut & hot water in a food processor to a coarse pulp.

▹ Put the coconut pulp into a square of cheesecloth, gather up the corners & strain the liquid into a saucepan squeezing the cheesecloth to get every drop. Discard pulp. Heat the liquid over medium-low heat & add the whole milk, sugar & salt. Simmer for 5 minutes.

▹ Pour the mixture into the molds. Add some of the coconut shavings to each mold. Cover & freeze for at least 5 hours.

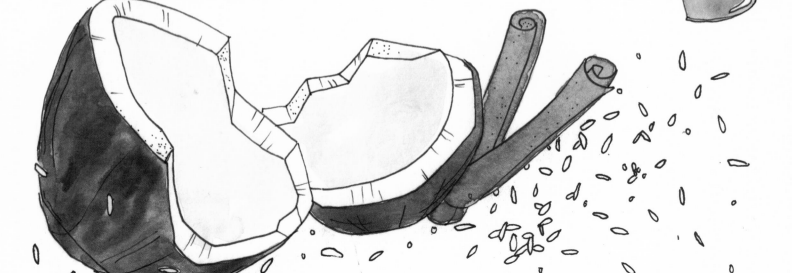

Higos en Almíbar con Queso

stewed figs with fresh cheese

serves 8   prep time: 3 hours

25 ripe figs
1 3/4 lb of panela (chunk of dense brown sugar)
3 cinnamon sticks
1 tbsp cloves

12 ounces queso fresco

① Wash figs, then cut in half.

② Boil figs in full pot of water for about 20 minutes or until soft.

③ Turn off heat, allow figs to soak for one hour, then drain.

PREPARING THE ALMÍBAR: Heat panela, cinnamon sticks & cloves in 6 cups water.

Simmer on stove until panela is dissolved.

Combine figs & almíbar, cook on low heat for about 1½ hours. Almíbar will reduce, turning into a true syrup.

Serve one or two figs & almíbar over 2"×2"×½" pieces of queso fresco.

flan

serves 6

· 1½ cups sugar
· 2 tbsp water
· juice from ½ lemon
· 3 cups heavy cream
· 1 tsp vanilla extract
· 5 eggs
· ½ tsp cinnamon

Variations: add other flavors such as rum or almond extract.

① Place 6 single-serve molds in baking pan ½ full of hot water.

② Cook 1 cup sugar in heavy saucepan with 2 tbsp water on medium-high heat. Heat slowly, tilting saucepan back & forth to melt sugar. In about 10 minutes, sugar should caramelize. Continue to tilt pot rather than stir. Be careful not to burn, which can happen quickly. Add lemon juice.

③ Pour mixture into each flan mold, coating the bottom surface with an ⅛" glaze of caramel.

④ Preheat the oven to 325°. Heat the cream on medium low & add vanilla extract. Stir. (5 min)

⑤ Beat eggs with ½ cup sugar & cinnamon. Then slowly pour heavy cream in while stirring. Strain mixture as you pour flan batter into each mold.

⑥ Bake flan for 40-50 minutes in baking pan ½ full of water (baño de maria).

⑦ Flan has a thin smooth glaze on surface when finished baking. Chill for at least 4 hours or overnight.

⑧ To serve, cut around edge & place plate on top. Flip. Remove bowl. Allow caramel to settle around flan.

Alfajores

A delicious sandwich cookie from Argentina

My friend Wes who makes alfajores regularly to sell explains that the goal is to create a crumbly cookie that is not dry, but flaky & sweet.

Held together by Dulce de Leche, it's the ultimate treat!

THE DOUGH

- ▷ 1 cup cornstarch
- ▷ 3/4 cup all-purpose flour + more as needed.
- ▷ 1 tsp baking powder
- ▷ 1/2 tsp baking soda
- ▷ 1/4 tsp fine salt

- ▷ 8 tbsp unsalted butter (1 stick), room temperature
- ▷ 1/3 cup granulated sugar
- ▷ 2 large egg yolks
  - fresh eggs preferred for rich yellow color
- ▷ 1 tbsp pisco or brandy
- ▷ 1/2 tsp vanilla extract

THE FILLING & TOPPING

- ▷ 12 oz Dulce de Leche*, at room temperature
  - 30 min. out of the fridge is good.
- ▷ 2 tbsp powdered sugar, for dusting on top.

Mix together cornstarch, 3/4 cup flour, baking powder, baking soda & salt; set aside.

Combine butter & sugar using a stand mixer & a paddle attachment. Mix on medium speed; stop the mixer to scrape down the bowl with a rubber spatula. Mix until the sugar is fully integrated & mixture appears fluffy (3 min.).

In a separate bowl, whisk together the egg yolks, pisco or brandy & vanilla.

Add this mixture to butter & sugar & mix on medium speed (1 min.).

On low speed, add the flour bit by bit to the bowl, stopping the mixer as needed to scrape down the sides. Mix until there are no visible flour pockets. (1-2 min.)

Remove the dough from the mixer & shape it into a disk. Wrap tightly with plastic wrap & chill in refrigerator for at least 30 minutes.

Chilling the dough makes the dough easier to work with & cookies don't spread out so much when baking.

Heat the oven to 350°F & line a baking sheet with parchment paper. Place the chilled dough on a lightly floured surface. Lightly flour the top of the dough & roll to 1/4" thickness. Stamp out as many rounds as possible using a 2" round cutter (the mouth of an 8 oz canning jar will work too). Reroll the dough as necessary until all of it has been used. Yields 22-24 rounds.

Place the cookies on the prepared baking sheet, 1/2" apart & bake until golden on the bottom but still pale on top. (12-14 min). Transfer to wire rack.

Spoon the dulce de leche into a pastry bag. Or, use a resealable plastic bag & cut off a 1/4" hole in a corner.

Flip half of the cookies upside down. Pipe about 1 1/2 teaspoons of the dulce de leche on each. Place a second cookie on top & gently press down, creating a sandwich.

Using a fine wire colander, dust the cookies generously with powdered sugar.

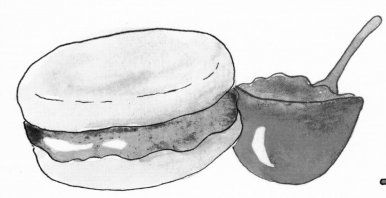

DULCE de LECHE

A caramel-like sweet made from Milk & Sugar

There are many variations of Dulce de Leche throughout Latin America, including:

CAJETA: A Mexican version made of half goat's milk & half cow's milk; always made in a copper pot & named after the original small wooden boxes it was packed in.

CORTADA: Common in Cuban cuisine, has a lumpy texture, usually eaten by itself.

DULCE de LECHE en TABLA (tablet): Dominican style poured into molds to set for several hours; texture similar to fudge.

MANJAR BLANCO: Popular in Peru, Chile & Ecuador & eaten on ice cream or with bizcocho cookies

Here's the EASIEST way to make DULCE de LECHE:

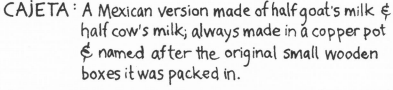

INGREDIENTS: 1 can of sweetened condensed milk. That's it!

1. Remove the paper label from the can.

2. Fill a pot with water.

3. Place the can in the water.

4. Cover the pot & bring the water to a boil.

5. Lower heat & simmer for 4 hours, refilling the pot with water as needed, so that the can is completely covered with water at all times. (This is important because if not, the pressure may not be equally distributed inside the can & it could explode.)

6. Using tongs, take the can out of the water & let it cool completely before opening. The can may bulge because it is under pressure.

7. When can is cool, open it & enjoy! To store, transfer the dulce de leche to an airtight container & refrigerate.

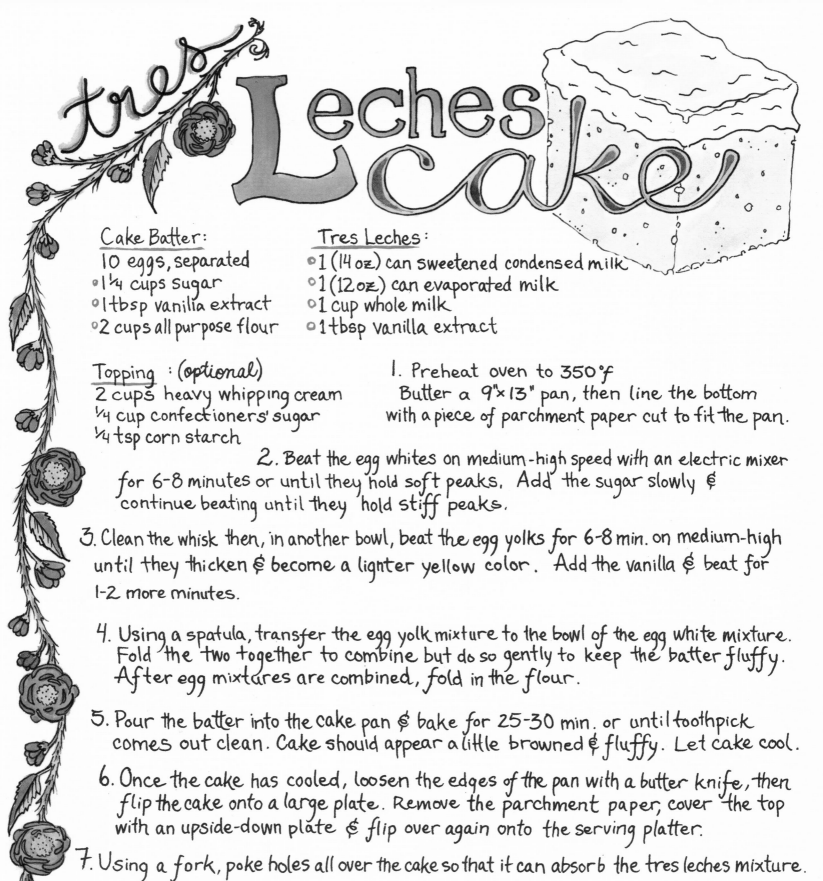

Tres Leches Cake

Cake Batter:
- 10 eggs, separated
- 1¼ cups sugar
- 1 tbsp vanilla extract
- 2 cups all purpose flour

Tres Leches:
- 1 (14 oz) can sweetened condensed milk
- 1 (12 oz) can evaporated milk
- 1 cup whole milk
- 1 tbsp vanilla extract

Topping : (optional)
- 2 cups heavy whipping cream
- ¼ cup confectioners' sugar
- ¼ tsp corn starch

1. Preheat oven to 350°f
   Butter a 9"x13" pan, then line the bottom with a piece of parchment paper cut to fit the pan.

2. Beat the egg whites on medium-high speed with an electric mixer for 6-8 minutes or until they hold soft peaks. Add the sugar slowly & continue beating until they hold stiff peaks.

3. Clean the whisk then, in another bowl, beat the egg yolks for 6-8 min. on medium-high until they thicken & become a lighter yellow color. Add the vanilla & beat for 1-2 more minutes.

4. Using a spatula, transfer the egg yolk mixture to the bowl of the egg white mixture. Fold the two together to combine but do so gently to keep the batter fluffy. After egg mixtures are combined, fold in the flour.

5. Pour the batter into the cake pan & bake for 25-30 min. or until toothpick comes out clean. Cake should appear a little browned & fluffy. Let cake cool.

6. Once the cake has cooled, loosen the edges of the pan with a butter knife, then flip the cake onto a large plate. Remove the parchment paper, cover the top with an upside-down plate & flip over again onto the serving platter.

7. Using a fork, poke holes all over the cake so that it can absorb the tres leches mixture.

8. Whisk together the sweetened condensed milk, evaporated milk, whole milk & vanilla extract until well combined. Pour evenly over the cake.

9. Clean the whisk of the mixer & whip the heavy cream with the confectioners' sugar & cornstarch until it holds up stiff peaks (3 min). Spread the whipped cream all over the cake. *Enjoy!*

PUERTO RICAN MALLORCA

I first ate this bread with my cousin in Puerto Rico. Sitting in a little diner on red swivel stools, we sipped our late morning coffee & munched on sweet mallorca, an Island favorite.

1 Combine yeast, 1 cup water & 1 tbsp sugar.

2 In a separate bowl, combine 1¾ sticks of the butter, egg yolks, 4 cups flour, milk, remaining sugar, orange zest & salt. Add yeast mixture & mix well.

3 Lightly flour surface & knead for 5 mins, adding flour so dough does not become sticky.

4 Grease bowl, add dough, let rise in a warm area. (45 mins)

When dough has doubled in size, punch it down! Separate into 10 pieces, equal size.

5 Make long snakes, roll them into flat spirals. Place onto greased baking sheet.

Let rise (1 hour)

6 Brush with remaining 2 tbsp melted butter.

7 Bake at 375°F. (20-30min)

8 Let cool (5 min). Sprinkle powdered sugar on top.

Ingredients

3/4 tsp SALT
1 cup MILK
1 cup lukewarm WATER
1 package active dry YEAST
Zest FROM ONE ORANGE
5 cups FLOUR
3/4 cup SUGAR
2 STICKS melted BUTTER unsalted
6 EGG YOLKS

PLATANOS Maduros Fritos

PREP TIME 20 MIN, SERVES 4

- 2-3 ripe plantains (dark brown maduros)
- ⅓ cup frying oil or butter
- ¼ cup sugar, brown or white

1. Peel ripe plantains (maduros) & cut diagonally into 1" slices.
2. Heat oil or butter in pan over medium heat.
3. Lightly coat the maduro slices with a little sugar.
4. Fry the maduros for about 1 minute on each side.
5. Reduce heat to low so they can caramelize, turning a golden brown color (3 minutes).
6. Blot maduros with a paper towel.

Enjoy immediately!

Cocadas

This soft, chewy coconut cookie is found in a variety of shapes & natural or dyed colors. Cocadas can usually be found in the coastal regions of Latin America where coconuts are abundant. This one is from Mexico.

- 3½ cups shredded sweetened coconut
- 3/4 cup sweetened condensed milk OR 3/4 cup dulce de leche.
- 1½ tsp vanilla extract
- 2 egg whites
- pinch of sea salt

1. Preheat the oven to 375°f. Line a baking sheet with parchment paper.

2. Mix together the coconut, sweetened condensed milk or dulce de leche, vanilla extract & egg whites.

3. Form tablespoons of dough into balls & arrange 2" apart on the lined baking sheet. Sprinkle a pinch of salt on top of each.

4. Bake until the edges & tops of the cocadas are golden brown, 12-15 mins. Remove from the oven & cool for 10 mins on baking sheet, allowing them to firm up before moving to a wire rack to cool completely.

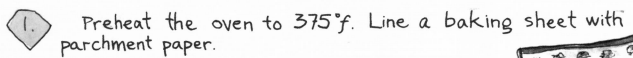

129

Glossary

Achiote (annatto)... A seed used as a natural colorant for dishes including rice & potatoes.

Ají..... Hot chile pepper from the Andean part of South America.

Ají Amarillo..... medium hot, slightly citrusy chile pepper. An essential in Peruvian cuisine

Almíbar...... A syrup made from a sweetener & warm water.

Avocado leaves... Enjoy fresh or dried. Flavor is similar to anise but stronger.

Ayocote Beans... An heirloom pinto bean from Central America.

Baño de Maria... A water bath to heat food gently. (bain marie)

Bomba..... A short grain Paella rice from Calasparra, Spain.

Camarón...... Shrimp. Gamba in some parts of South America.

Capsicum... Genus of flowering plant in the nightshade family, native to the Americas. The fruit is called a pepper.

Ceviche..... Coastal dish made of seafood "cooked" by citrus juice.

Chayote.... A vegetable native to Brazil. Has a mild flavor similar to squash.

Chile......... Fruit of the genus capsicum.

Chile de Árbol.... A small potent Mexican chile also known as bird's beak chile.

Chulpe...... An Andean corn for toasting. *Chulpe is similar to Corn Nuts.*

131

 Comida Latina...Food from Central & South America as well as the Caribbean.

 Comál........A smooth, flat griddle typically used to cook tortillas.

Cracked corn...Broken up dried corn kernels. *I use this to make morocho*

 Curtido......A type of cabbage relish, sometimes lightly fermented.

Deveining......Removing white membrane inside a chile, or remnants of the intestines in a shrimp or large prawn.

Epazote......An herb native to Central & South America. Flavor is similar to fennel or tarragon but stronger.

Fine Strainer...Perforated steel mesh (1/16"), kitchen tool used to separate solids & to drain excess liquid.

Flake (fish)...To loosely break apart flesh with a fork.

Flan mold....4 ounce ramekin or small ceramic bowl.

Guajillo chile. A variety of chile pepper produced by drying mirasol chiles. Deep red in color.

Harina........Flour.

Hominy (see Mote)

Julienne......Culinary knife cut where the food is cut into long thin strips similar to matchsticks.

 Kitchen scrub..A sponge used to scour dishes, helpful for removing spines, scales & the like.

 Lard..........Rendered Pork fat.

 Llapingacho...Ecuadorian dish consisting of potato pancakes stuffed with cheese, cooked until crisp.

Majado.......Mashed.

Mandoline....A cooking utensil used for slicing.

Masa Harina...A pre-cooked corn meal.

Masarepa....... A pre-cooked cornmeal used in
Masa al instante Venezuela & Colombia to make arepas
Arepa flour   (plump tortilla). Not treated with lime.

Membrillo...A sweet, dense jelly made of quince, similar to dulce de guayaba (guava paste).

Mirasol.....A thin-skinned chile pepper; guajillo in dried form.

 Molinillo....A Mexican kitchen tool used to prepare atole (corn-based beverage) or hot chocolate.

Morocho....A variety of dried corn. Ecuadorians make a hot drink with morocho.

 Mortar [&]...A hard bowl   } together used for
Pestle......A heavy club-shaped object} crushing & grinding.

Mote (hominy). Large kernel corn that has been soaked in an alkaline solution.

Nixtamalization...Process for the preparation of corn or grain where the grain is soaked in an alkaline solution, usually lime water.

Nopales.....Edible leaf/pad segments of the opuntia cactus.

Panela/piloncillo..A molded unrefined brown sugar.

Paring knife...Small knife with a plain edge blade ideal for peeling, deveining or seeding.

Plantain/Plátano....A starchy banana eaten green or ripe.
(Verde or Maduro)

Posole...... A traditional Mexican soup including a large kernel corn.

Queso Cotija..A salty cow's milk cheese.

Refrescos....Cold beverages, refreshments.

Salsa.......A sauce.

Sofrito.......An essential flavor base of onions, garlic, spices & sometimes peppers.

Sugar cane...Cane is used in the production of sugar & eaten raw in countries throughout Latin America.

Tamales.....A traditional Central American dish made of a starchy dough, usually corn, which is steamed in a leaf wrapper.

Tamarind.....Pod-like fruit from the Tamarindus Indica
Tamarindo   tree. The sour pulp is common in juices
             & sauces in Mexico. Find in a Latin
             American grocery as a dried pod or paste.

Tomar.......To drink.

Tomate de Árbol.. Red or yellow, flesh is acidic & tart
(tree tomato)   & common in sauces & juices in Ecuador
OR Tamarillo   & Colombia. Pulp can be bought frozen
                 in many Latin American groceries.

Tomatillos....Plant in the nightshade family related to
              cape gooseberry. Fruit is surrounded
              by inedible paper-like husk.

Tomato
Tomate......A tomatillo in Mexico.
Jitomate....A red tomato in Mexico.

Tortilla Press..Tool used to make tortillas in Mexico.
                Essential for making lots of equally thick,
                round tortillas at home.

Tunas.......The fruit of the prickly pear cactus,
            or Opuntia.

Yuca......Cassava. Tuber native to South America.

Zapallo......Small pumpkin or winter squash.

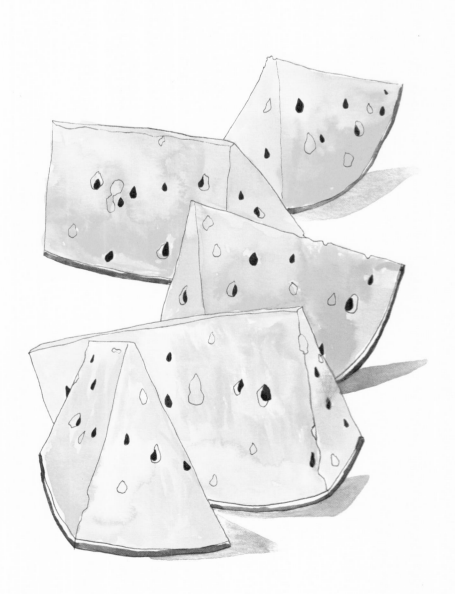

index

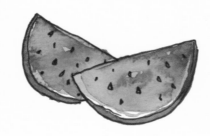

THANK YOU SO MUCH for your guidance, SUPPORT & encouragement, you inspire me! I COULDN'T HAVE made this book without YOU ♥

Marc Pfeuffer
Jeannae Flores
Marco Vinicio Fiallo
Ken Neubaker
Kate Winslow
Tricia McCauley
Whitney Cookman
Dean Hively
Lili Herrera
Greg Upwall

Pedro Proaño
Jeff Fox
Wesley Tahsir
Rosa Sanabria
Buzz Teacher
Bryan Simmons
Janet Teacher
Woody Pollock
Jorie Partridge
Hunter Sunrise
Christopher Graham
Leslie Atkins
Charlene Murdock
Rachel Cohen Marshall
Laura Westmeyer
Marco Julio & Alicia Fiallo
Marico Jayne
Juan Sebastián Pérez
Micah Beard
Sylvia Tan
Paulina Kriebel
Greg Kriebel
Dustin Kriebel
alejandra Proaño
Lorenz Wild

Marcella Kriebel is an artist best known for her watercolor illustration. She holds a degree in Studio Art & Cultural Anthropology from Willamette University & sells her work through a variety of online venues including Etsy.com. Marcella is ever-expanding her portfolio through the execution of fresh projects including Art Every Day: 365 Days of Food, which can be viewed at marcellakriebel.com. In addition, Marcella has partnered with National Geographic to create art for National Food Day & has been featured on Food 52 & other culinary blogs. The independently published edition of this book was highlighted in the Washington Post's Best Cookbooks of 2013. Marcella shares her passions for food & art through digital & television media, demos at farmers markets, & by teaching classes that combine her loves -cooking & painting - & inspire others to connect with theirs as well.

photo: Leslie Atkins

Notas

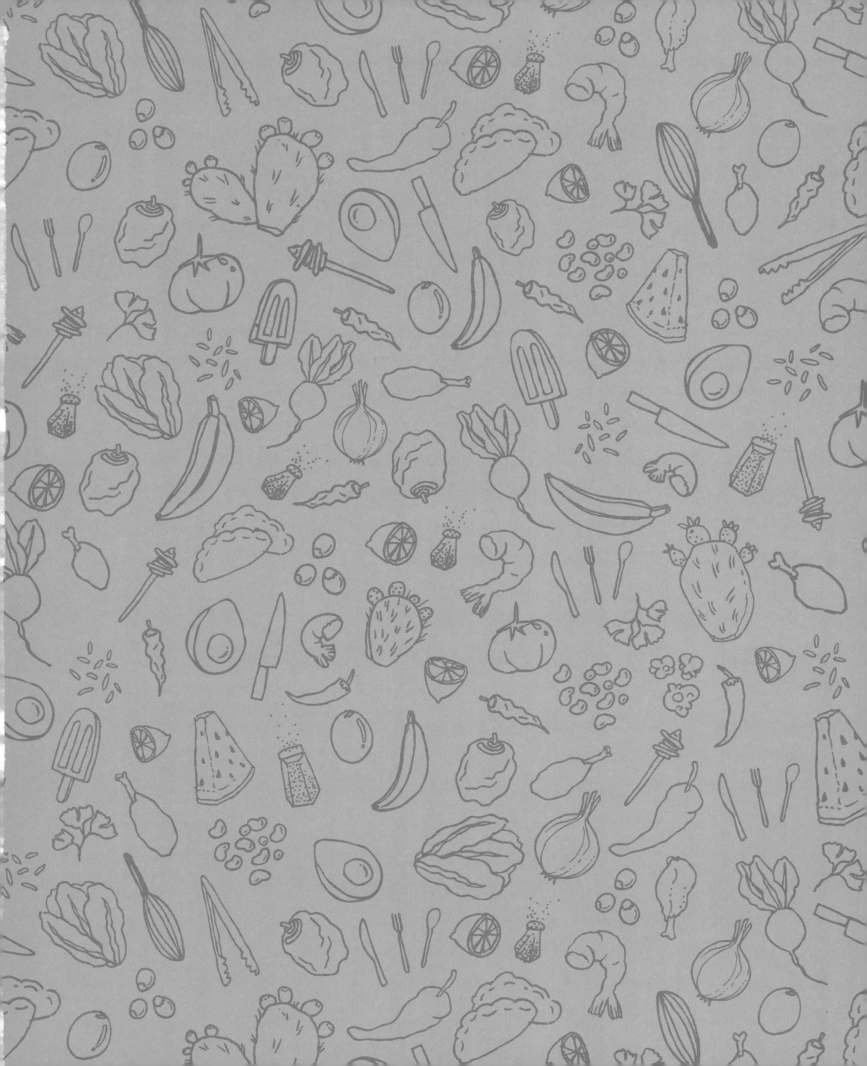

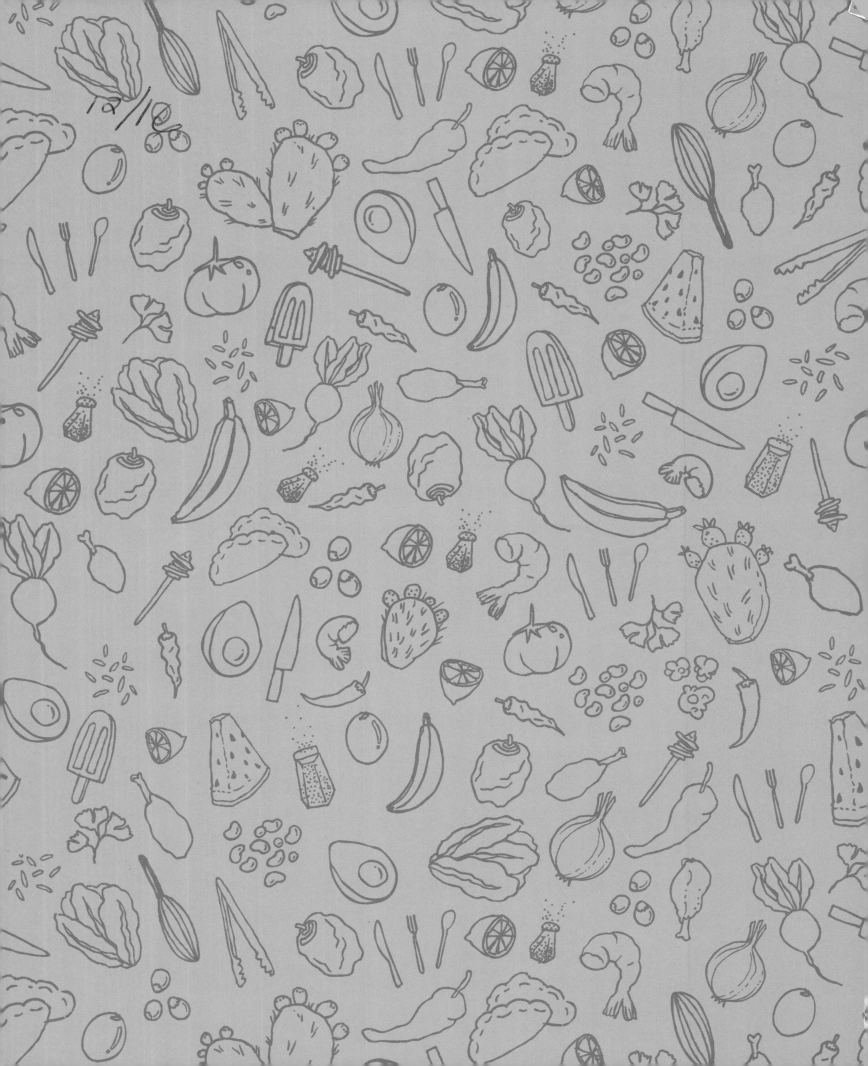